The Book of Church Order
of the Sovereign Grace Churches

The Book of Church Order
of the Sovereign Grace Churches

Eighth Edition • December 2018

The Book of Church Order of the Sovereign Grace Churches. 8th edition.
© 2018 by Sovereign Grace Churches, Inc.

Unless otherwise indicated, all Scripture quotations are from the ESV Bible (The Holy Bible, English Standard Version®), copyright© 2001 by Crossway, a publishing ministry of Good News Publishers. Used by permission. All rights reserved. Scripture quotations marked (ESV) are also from the ESV Bible. Scripture quotations marked (NASB) taken from the New American Standard Bible®, copyright© 1960, 1962, 1963, 1968, 1971, 1972, 1973, 1975, 1977, 1995 by The Lockman Foundation. Used by permission. www.Lockman.org. Scripture quotations marked (NIV) are taken from the Holy Bible, New International Version®, NIV®. Copyright© 1973, 1978, 1984, 2011 by Biblica, Inc.® Used by permission of Zondervan. Quotations designated (NET) are from the NET Bible® copyright ©1996-2016 by Biblical Studies Press, L.L.C. http://netbible.org All rights reserved. Scripture quotations marked (KJV) are from the King James Version Bible. Public Domain.

TABLE OF CONTENTS

PART ONE – GENERAL PRINCIPLES

1	General Principles	9

PART TWO – LOCAL CHURCH POLITY

2	The Office of Elder	15
	2.1 New Testament Terminology: Elder, Pastor, Overseer	15
	2.2 The Responsibilities of the Elder	16
3	Qualifications of Elders	18
4	The Elder as Christian *First*	26
5	Elders and Plurality	27
6	Bi-Vocational Elders	28
7	The Senior Pastor	30
	7.1 Terms "Lead Pastor," "Lead Elder," or "Senior Pastor"	30
	7.2 Repositioning of the Senior Pastor	30
8	Accountability for Pastors	34
9	The Ordination of Elders	36
	9.1 Introduction	36
	9.2 Feedback Throughout the Process	36
	9.3 The Basic Process for Ordination	37
	Pastor's College	38
	Pastoral Internship	38
	9.4 The Duration of the Office of Overseer	42
	9.5 Churches without Elders	43
	9.6 Exceptions to *Statement of Faith* or *Book of Church Order*	43
	9.7 Transfer of Ordination Status Within Sovereign Grace Churches	43
	9.8 Transfer of Ordination Status Across Denominations	45
10	The Office of Deacon	48
	10.1 Biblical Basis	48
	10.2 Characteristics of a Deacon	48
	10.3 Role of a Deacon	50
11	The Role of the Congregation	51
	11.1 Introduction	51
	11.2 Congregational Equality	52
	11.3 Congregational Solidarity	52
	11.4 Congregational Responsibility	53
	11.5 Congregational Submission	54

12	Local Church Practices		56
	12.1 Local Church Bylaws		56
	12.2 Official Membership		57
	12.3 Solemnization of Marriage		57
	12.4 Reporting Sexual Abuse of a Child		57

PART THREE – EXTR-LOCAL POLITY

13	Regional Assemblies of Elders		59
	13.1 Defining a Region		59
	13.2 Responsibilities of the Regional Assemblies of Elders		60
	Ordination and Exams		60
	Adjudications		61
	Discipline of an Eldership		62
	Church Planting		63
	Church Adoptions		64
	Regional Committees		67
	Selection of a Regional Leader		69
	Approval of Changes to the Sovereign Grace *Statement of Faith*		70
14	Regional Leaders		71
15	The Council of Elders		73
	15.1 Formation		73
	15.2 Annual and Special Meetings		73
	15.3 Responsibilities		74
	Polity Committee		75
	Theology Committee		76
	Changes to *Statement of Faith*		77
	Changes to *Book of Church Order*		79
	Changes to Ordination Standards		80
	15.4 Procedures for Council of Elders Meetings		81
	Rules Committee		82
16	Sovereign Grace Nominating Committee		83
17	The Executive Committee of the Council of Elders		85
18	Leadership Team		87
	18.1 Definition and Rationale		87
	18.2 Qualifications		87
	18.3 Responsibilities		87
	18.4 Personnel		89
	Executive Director		89

19	Partnership Agreements		92
	19.1	For Provisional Regions	92
	19.2	For United States Regions	98
	19.3	Partnership for Historic Sovereign Grace Churches without a Current Partnership Agreement	102
20	Process of Separation for a Local Church from Sovereign Grace		103
	20.1	General Principles	103
	20.2	Procedure	103
	20.3	Dissolving an Existing Church by the Local Elder(s) and the Regional Leader	105

PART FOUR – RULES OF DISCIPLINE

21	Principles of Discipline		107
22	Discipline in the Local Church		109
23	Discipline of a Church Member		111
24	Discipline of an Elder		113
	24.1	Gross or Scandalous Sins	114
	24.2	Requirements for bringing a charge	115
	24.3	Moderator of Just Cause Pretrial Procedures	118
	24.4	Plaintiff May Appeal Moderator's Decision	119
	24.5	The Panel	120
	24.6	The Rights of the Defendant	120
	24.7	The Rights of the Plaintiff	122
	24.8	Trial Proceedings	123
	24.9	Trial Results	126
	24.10	Process for Care and Restoration	128
	24.11	Communication	129
	24.12	Appeals	129
	24.13	Removal of an Elder(s) for Deficiencies	130
25	Regional Judicial Review Committees		131
	25.1	Appointment of the Judicial Review Committee	131
	25.2	Powers and Responsibilities	131
		Charges against Extra-Local Leaders	132
		Public Censure of an Eldership	133
		Disavowal of an Eldership	134
		Removal of a Church	135
26	The Sovereign Grace Court of Appeal		137
27	Revision History		139
28	Index of Key Topics		141

The Book of Church Order
of the Sovereign Grace Churches[1]

PART ONE: General Principles of the Sovereign Grace Churches[2]

1 General Principles

1.1 Jesus Christ has all authority in heaven and earth (Matt. 28:18), and he reigns as head over his church (Col. 1:18; Eph. 1:22), which he purchased with his own blood (Acts 20:28; Heb. 13:12). All authority in the church derives from him and is exercised on his behalf.

1.2 A local church consists of any body of baptized believers associated together for the worship of God and for carrying out Christ's commission to disciple the nations (Matt. 28:19-20). The church's worship essentially includes the preaching of the Word, the administration of the sacraments of baptism and the Lord's Supper, and the maintenance of corporate holiness through discipline. It also includes the singing of songs, hymns, and spiritual songs and the exercise of the spiritual gifts for mutual edification.

1.3 Each Sovereign Grace church is an expression of the church universal and, as such, has an essential integrity as an authentic church. A local church does not depend for its essential identity as a church of Jesus Christ upon its institutional affiliation with any other church. Each local church has the authority to govern its own affairs, call and ordain its own deacons and elders, and maintain its own holiness through church discipline as necessary.

1.4 The elders of each local church have sole responsibility to govern its affairs under the Lordship of Christ and the authority of Scripture. Churches without elders are governed according to BCO-9.5.

1.4.1 The terms "elder," "pastor/shepherd," and "overseer/bishop" all refer to one and the same office (Titus 1:5, 7; Acts 20:17, 28; 1 Pet. 5:1, 2).

1.4.2 While officers are not absolutely essential to the existence of a local church, they are necessary for its well-being (Acts 14:23-25; Titus 1:5; Eph. 4:11-16).

---

[1] There are several documents related to *The Book of Church Order* available on the main website of the Sovereign Grace Churches, Inc. These include theological and practical documents, summary explanations of *The Book of Church Order*, older versions of *The Book of Church Order*, and many of the appendices that were included in the First Edition of *The Book of Church Order*.

[2] In this document, "Sovereign Grace" will typically refer to the denomination officially called Sovereign Grace Churches, Inc. It is the ecclesiastical entity that is comprised of all those churches who have signed the Partnership Agreement (BCO-19). "Denomination" simply means a group of churches distinct in their faith and practice and typically joined together for mission, etc. Thus, it is equivalent to how we used "family of churches" in the past.

1.4.3   Each church should strive to have a plurality of elders, according to the biblical precedent and prescription (Acts 11:30; 13:1; 14:23; 15:2, 4, 6, 22-23; 16:4; 20:17; 21:18; 1 Tim. 5:17; Titus 1:5; Jas. 5:14; 1 Pet. 5:1). This priority, while biblical, is not absolute. The New Testament can envision a church without a plurality of elders, and the goal of plurality is balanced by the need to have qualified elders (1 Tim. 5:22).

1.4.4   Although elders have different gifts and roles (1 Cor. 12; Rom. 12:3-8; cf. 1 Cor. 3:5-9; Luke 19:11-27), all must meet the same qualifications because all occupy the same office (1 Tim. 3:1-7; Titus 1:5-9), which essentially involves ruling and teaching (1 Tim. 3:2; cf. 2 Tim. 2:24; Titus 1:9).

1.4.5   Since all elders occupy the same office, they have equal authority and act as a body (Acts 13:1-3; 15:22-23).

1.4.6   Elders ought to receive compensation (1 Cor. 9:6-14; Luke 10:7/Matt 10:10), and congregations have a correlative duty to pay them if possible (Gal. 6:6; 1 Tim. 5:17-18).

1.4.7   Elders, as under-shepherds of Christ (1 Pet. 5:1-4), must serve as examples, teach sound doctrine, guard against false doctrine, care for the spiritual well-being of the church, govern the affairs of the church, equip the church for ministry, and raise up future leadership.

1.4.8   Apostles and elders governed the churches of the New Testament. Sovereign Grace churches allow for the belief in modern-day apostles or apostolic leadership without requiring it or explicitly featuring it in their polity. Sovereign Grace churches recognize the office of elder as continuing today. The office of deacon continues as well but is not a governing office. Some of the non-authoritative functions of apostles are carried out by Regional Leaders and the members of the Leadership Team.

1.4.9   Church members do not have an inferior status to elders, but are equal in standing before Christ and fellow members of his body. All members of the church—elders and congregants—are sheep under the authority of the Chief Shepherd, submitted to God's Word. All possess the same privileges of adoption by God, redemption by Christ, and filling of the Holy Spirit. Church members also have vital responsibilities that contribute to the life and mission of the church.

1.4.10 In addition to their vital role and many privileges, church members are called to submit to their elders in church affairs (1 Thess. 5:12-13; Heb. 13:17; 1 Pet. 5:5), assuming that elders are faithfully teaching and leading in accordance with God's Word, which circumscribes their authority.

1.4.11 The responsibility to receive and excommunicate church members belongs to the church as a whole (Matt. 18:18-20) but is specifically given to the church's governing officers to exercise in leadership of the congregation (Matt. 16:18-19; John 20:23; 1 Cor. 4:14-5:13; 2 Cor. 13:1-

4). In addition to a full array of other mutual responsibilities (e.g., love, encouragement, care, etc.), congregants are obliged to lovingly confront one another for impenitent sin (Matt. 18:15-16). Governing officers are authorized to hear such charges and render a verdict which they pronounce on behalf of the whole church and in its presence, in the name and power of Jesus Christ, as a corporate appeal for the sinner to repent (Matt. 18:17, 20; 1 Cor. 4:19-21; 5:4-5). Congregants have the duty to carry out the discipline of an excommunicated person by relating to him/her as an unbeliever (1 Cor. 5:9-13; 2 Cor. 2:6; 2 Thess. 3:6, 14-15). Governing officers also decide when to readmit the penitent to the fellowship of the church (2 Cor. 2:6-8). It is the duty of the congregants to forgive, comfort, and reaffirm their love for such a one (2 Cor. 2:7-8).

1.4.12 Congregants help to identify men in their midst who are qualified to serve as officers (Acts 1:23; 6:3a, 5). But only governing officers, with the counsel and support of the congregation, exercise the authority to select, ordain, and install church officers (Acts 6:3b, 6; Acts 14:23; 1 Tim. 3:1-13; 4:14; 5:22; 2 Tim. 2:2; Titus 1:5).

1.4.13 Congregants have the duty to bring charges against immoral or heterodox church officers (2 Cor. 11:4; 1 Tim. 5:19). Governing officers have the duty to adjudicate such charges and to pronounce public censure (1 Tim. 5:19-21).

1.5 Christ is the head of one body, the church universal, consisting of the elect saints of all ages who share the one hope, one Lord, one faith, one baptism, and one God and Father of all who is over all and through all and in all. Sovereign Grace local churches seek to give their spiritual unity in Christ as much concrete institutional expression as is practical. In this way we bear visible witness to our union under one head, Jesus Christ; we benefit from the gifts and wisdom of other leaders and members of the body of Christ; we increase our effectiveness in fulfilling the mission Christ has given to his church; we strive toward and protect the unity of the faith and of the knowledge of the Son of God; and thus the whole body, joined and held together by every joint with which it is equipped, when each part is working properly, grows up into mature manhood.

1.6 Moreover, no local church is omnicompetent or self-sufficient to carry out the mission which Christ has entrusted to the entire church (Matt. 28:19-20). Each local body stands in need of other local bodies in a relationship of interdependence.

1.7 This interdependence is more adequately expressed when local churches associate together in wider ecclesiastical bodies with shared resources, mission, mutual care, support, edification, and cooperation in government. Such cooperation is necessary for the protection of doctrinal fidelity and standards of holiness, the direction of a common mission, and the disposal of common funds. The members of an ecclesiastical body bear a substantial degree of corporate responsibility for the holiness and welfare of the whole.

1.8 Therefore the elders of local churches are accountable for their life and doctrine, not only to their own local congregations, but also in part to the broader ecclesiastical body as represented by her officers. The authority a local eldership exercises over its local congregation should not be an absolute authority without further appeal or recourse.

1.9 The Sovereign Grace churches express these principles of spiritual unity primarily through the Regional Assemblies of Elders and the Council of Elders. These bodies advance the mission by administrating church planting, pastoral training and theological education, and ordination standards. Through the actions of these bodies, the churches share material and spiritual resources with one another. The Regional Assemblies of Elders and the Council of Elders also help maintain the integrity of our corporate witness through the exercise of specified extra-local functions. These assemblies, to which elders agree to hold themselves accountable, serve as a protection to local congregations. They additionally perform a vital and necessary function in the process of the ordination of elders, their censure, judging their qualification for office, and other judicial functions detailed below in the Rules of Discipline. Each church maintains control over its own property and physical assets in accordance with its bylaws and does not relinquish such control by joining an ecclesiastical union.

1.10 The Sovereign Grace churches comprise an ecclesiastical body, significantly bound together in a common confession of faith, pursuing a common mission, guarding the corporate holiness of all the members, and governed by the assembly of the elders.

    1.10.1 Every church or association of particular churches is entitled to determine the terms for admission into its communion, the qualifications of its pastors, and the workings of its internal government as long as these are in compliance with the Word of God. Sovereign Grace Churches, based upon mutual love and confidence, has voluntarily determined to approve and appropriate the Sovereign Grace *Statement of Faith*, *Partnership Agreement*, and *Book of Church Order* as governing statutes and guidelines ordering their fellowship locally and with other Sovereign Grace churches. This genuine union among Sovereign Grace Churches carries with it all the rights and privileges due to each Sovereign Grace local church. This union is in effect for a member church once its elders have signed the appropriate Partnership Agreement (cf. BCO-19) and it has been accepted and approved by its Regional Assembly of Elders.[3]

    1.10.2 Yet union and fellowship within an ecclesiastical body is much more than a temporary means toward receiving the benefits of such a union. Union

---

[3] These privileges include the support and protection provided by the Regional Assemblies of Elders, participation in and protection by the Council of Elders, access to specialized theological training through the Sovereign Grace Pastors College, training that occurs in our various conferences, certain websites and online discussions, financial help for church planting, and all the benefits that result from our shared life as defined by this Book of Church Order and other Sovereign Grace documents.

carries with it both benefit and responsibility. Though at present it is not feasible to attain universal doctrinal and ecclesiastical unity within the body of Christ, it is commendable to tangibly demonstrate the reality of the love of God for his Son, his church, and his people by uniting and remaining in bona fide fellowship with other like-minded Christian congregations.

1.10.3 Sovereign Grace's polity gives tangible expression to God's command to pursue doctrinally substantiated unity and love (John 17:20-23) by connecting congregations to a broader ecclesiastical body of affiliated churches. Therefore, just as a church or an individual should not enter into a fellowship of churches lightly, so they should not leave a fellowship of churches in a casual way. Disassociation often conveys a false message about the bonds of Christian love. Christian churches have a responsibility to *work* for unity (see Phil. 2:2, 4:2; 1 Cor. 1:10; Eph. 4:3, 12-13) within their formalized affiliations both locally and extra-locally (1 Cor. 1:2). One way that commitment to Christ and his church can be expressed is by willingly yoking oneself to other like-minded churches and determining to remain in affectionate fellowship unless matters of conscience or doctrinal infidelity prevent such association. The same sobriety and reticence that should mark a decision by Sovereign Grace to remove a church should be present if a local congregation contemplates terminating its partnership and interconnectedness to the broader ecclesiastical body. Furthermore, any local church considering disassociation should consider not only the benefits it will forfeit, but the gifts it will deprive the wider ecclesiastical body of by such an acute action. The privilege of association (which includes doctrinal and moral accountability and continued fellowship in an organization of churches expressing the unity and love of Christ) takes precedence over issues of convenience, preference, difficult circumstances, an unwillingness to make minor concessions over tertiary matters, or a position of unqualified independence. In protecting the reputation of Christ, every church should make a concerted, vigorous, and lasting effort to maintain the unity of the Spirit in the bond of peace, modeling the love of Christ in its given communion of churches by only withdrawing from such fellowship due to exceptional circumstances.

1.11 We affirm that the visible church is the only organization on earth explicitly commissioned and equipped by Christ to disciple the nations. No other parachurch organization has been thus commissioned and equipped as the church of Jesus Christ. Because the visible church should not substantially delegate its mission to another organization, Sovereign Grace Churches, Inc., is therefore intentionally organized as an instrument of the Sovereign Grace churches that helps to facilitate their cooperation in relationship and a common mission. Its Executive Committee, Leadership Team, and employees occupy no higher or different church office than any other elders. As men endowed with a range of gifts to provide leadership to the church in its broader mission, the Directors and members of the Executive Committee are commissioned to such unique tasks by the Sovereign Grace elders to whom they are accountable. They have no special authority in the churches other than that which has been specifically delegated to them by the elders.

1.12 We affirm that Sovereign Grace exists to promote the shared values of:

- Reformed soteriology
- Gospel-centered expository preaching
- Continuationist pneumatology
- Complementarian leadership in the home and church
- Elder-governed and -led churches
- National and international outreach and church planting
- Interdependent churches united in fellowship, mission, and governance

1.13 *The Book of Church Order* defines the structure and key values of our gospel partnership together in Sovereign Grace Churches. Subscription to *The Book of Church Order* requires elders to comply with what it explicitly mandates and refrain from what it explicitly forbids, while operating in Biblical wisdom according to Sovereign Grace values in all other matters. *The Book of Church Order* does not provide detailed direction for every action we take in the normal course of our life together, but it does provide values that guide us and specific direction for some crucial decision points.

PART TWO: Local Church Polity

2 The Office of Elder

2.1 New Testament Terminology: Elder, Pastor, Overseer

From the beginning, local churches have been governed and led by elders (Acts 14:23; 1 Tim. 3:1-7; Titus 1:5-9) with the assistance of deacons (Acts 6:1-6; 1 Tim. 3:8-13).

Elder, Pastor, Overseer

The elder is ordained in a church to lead, teach, care for, and protect that local church. While we most often use the term "elder" for the pastoral office of the church, this is only one of several terms used in the New Testament to describe the role. The Bible refers interchangeably to this office as "elder," "pastor" (or "shepherd"), and "overseer."

"Elder" comes from the Greek *presbuteros* (e.g., 1 Tim. 5:1). When used of the office in the church, the implication is that the man is a mature and wise man, not necessarily that he has reached a certain age (1 Tim. 4:12).

A second term used of elders in the New Testament is "pastor" or "shepherd" (Gr., *poimēn*) as in Ephesians 4:11, "He gave the apostles, the prophets, the evangelists, the shepherds and teachers" (cf. John 21:16; Acts 20:28; 1 Pet. 5:1-4). Places like John 10 and Psalm 23 remind us of the specific, individual care that God extends to us as our "Good Shepherd" and model for us what is meant by the term as it is applied to the elders of a local church.

A third term is "overseer" (Gr., *episkopos*) as in 1 Timothy 3:1: "If anyone aspires to the office of overseer, he desires a noble task" (cf. Acts 20:28; Phil. 1:1; Titus 1:7). This term captures the authority and leadership entrusted to elders.

It is critical that we see the equivalence of these three terms in the New Testament: an elder is a pastor is an overseer. We can see the synonymous nature of the terms in Titus 1:5-9 where Titus is told to "appoint elders" (v. 5), and then he is instructed concerning potential candidates: "the overseer…must be" (v. 7). Further, in Acts 20:28 the Ephesian "elders" (20:17) are told how they must "shepherd" their flock as "overseers." In 1 Peter 5:1-4 he addresses "elders" (v. 1) and tells them to "shepherd the flock of God that is among you" (v. 2), specifically by "exercising oversight" (v. 2). While verb forms are mixed with the noun "elder" here, the ideas of elder-shepherd-overseer are clearly coextensive.

Thus, we ought to use all three terms to refer to the same office. Further, we need to let our understanding of the pastoral office include the connotations of all three terms. We cannot let one term swallow up the other two. Thus, the leadership and authority implied by "overseer" is to be joined to the protection, care, and nourishment implied by the use of "pastor"; and both of these are to be attached to the wisdom and mature discernment implied by the term "elder." The Bible itself must guide our use of these different terms, not how they have become traditionally understood in certain denominations.

2.2 The Responsibilities of the Elder

The elder-pastor-overseer has four broad responsibilities within the local church. Elders feed, oversee, care for, and protect the flock entrusted to them.

2.2.1 First, pastors are to "feed" the flock entrusted to their care (John 21:15).

Elders are "teachers" (Eph. 4:11) who build the church in their care by "preaching and teaching" (1 Tim. 5:17). This is why an elder must be "able to teach" (1 Tim. 3:2). Teaching happens through the ministry of the Word on Sunday mornings but also in the more private "reproof…correction…training" (2 Tim. 3:16), and exhortation (4:2) that happens in the pastor's ministry to individuals.

2.2.2 Second, elders are to oversee the flock entrusted to them (1 Tim. 3:1).

Elders provide leadership and thus manage "God's church" (1 Tim. 3:4-5). This leadership requirement is seen by the use of the title "overseers" to describe an elder (Acts 20:28; Phil. 1:1; 1 Tim. 3:1-2; Titus 1:7). Further, the use of the term "manage" in 1 Timothy 3:5 and the reference to "ruling" (Gr., *proistēmi*) in 1 Timothy 5:17 also support the notion that elders govern the church in a leadership capacity (cf. Rom. 12:8; 1 Thess. 5:12; etc.). Hebrews 13:17, which uses the more general term "leaders" (participle from *ēgeomai*, "lead, guide"), commands Christians to "obey your leaders and submit to them, for they are keeping watch over your souls," which seems to provide corroboration regarding the management and governing responsibilities of elders. Additionally, 1 Peter 5:2 reminds pastors that they are to be those "exercising oversight, not under compulsion."

2.2.3 Third, pastors are to care sincerely for the flock entrusted to them by God (Acts 20:28).

Just as the great commandments are to love God and to love our neighbor (Matt. 22:36-40), and apart from love we accomplish nothing and are nothing (1 Cor. 13:1-3), so a shepherd must "be genuinely concerned" for the "welfare" of every member of his respective church, not seeking his own interests, but "those of Jesus Christ" (Phil. 2:19-21).

2.2.4 Fourth, elders protect the flock, looking out for "wolves" that can come from without or within the church (Acts 20:28-30).

Elders are to "pay careful attention" and to "be alert" (vv. 28, 30). This is not to give an elder a suspicious heart, but a watchful one; not a cynical heart, but a cautious one. For example, the elder must know the difference between someone who disagrees with him and a divisive man who is actually a "wolf" (Rom. 16:17-18; Titus 3:10). Such attentiveness and discernment is part of the role.

3 Qualifications for Elders

Elders are to be men of exemplary character and adequate gifting. Many of the qualifications detailed for elders are *commanded* of all Christian men, implying the primacy of the elder's example. The difference with elders is that these qualifications are mandatory for office. The New Testament gives a number of requirements for elders, many of which do not appear in a list, e.g., he is to invest in and raise up future leaders (2 Tim. 2:2), to grow in his handling of God's Word (2 Tim. 2:15), to patiently endure evil (2 Tim. 2:24), etc. However, Paul provides the basic profile of an elder in the qualifications listed in 1 Timothy 3 and Titus 1, which are as follows:

3.1 Men

The New Testament is explicit that elders are to be men (1 Tim. 3:2; Titus 1:6; cf. 1 Tim 2:12).

3.2 Spiritual Maturity

Elders must have a sincere and mature faith in Christ, a connotation of the term "elder" (1 Tim. 3:6).

The Bible warns against allowing recent converts to occupy the office of elder because of the danger of pride and the temptations that might accompany pastoral ministry for an immature believer.

3.3 Exemplary Character

Pastors must be men of authentic and exemplary Christian character (1 Tim. 3:1-7; Titus 1:5-9), though they are not sinless (1 John 1:8-10).

Elders are called to be godly men. Their role as examples to the church and the temptations that accompany this office make it essential to have men of character perform this service. However, godliness does not equal sinlessness (see 1 John 1:8-10). Elders will not be perfect, though they must still be "above reproach" in the general sense. To call an elder "above reproach" is not to say that he is without fault, but rather, that he cannot be charged with any significant pattern of sin or especially heinous sin that will bring shame to the church or the gospel and ultimately undermine his pastoral ministry.

1 Timothy 3:1-7 and Titus 1:5-9 give the clearest pictures of what kind of man the elder is to be. We will summarize those requirements here.

3.3.1 "Above reproach" (1 Tim. 3:2; Titus 1:6) and "holy" (Titus 1:8)

The elder's life must not have obvious flaws that make his life open to the charge of hypocrisy, bring shame to the gospel, or would make the temptations that go along with the office of elder too great for him. He is one whom others would call "holy" in the basic, observable, but relative way that all fallen men can be holy.

3.3.2 "The husband of one wife" (1 Tim. 3:2; Titus 1:6)

The requirement here does not speak to whether a man has been divorced or remarried, but, if he is married, speaks to a general faithfulness and sexual purity in his current marriage. He is a "one woman kind of man." Of course, a man's marital history is relevant to establish his character, but his marital history is not primarily in view in these verses.

3.3.3 "Sober-minded" (1 Tim. 3:2)

The thought here is a clear-headedness that leads to rational thinking in difficult situations. The potential overseer must have the ability to see people in a variety of situations and not make rash judgments. Further, the elder must demonstrate a basic wisdom and insight into the human heart. The elder should possess the ability to encounter sin without being surprised and without growing cynical.

3.3.4 "Self-controlled" (1 Tim. 3:2; Titus 1:8) and "disciplined" (Titus 1:8)

Having "control of oneself" has relevance in all areas of life, such as finances, sexual purity, decision making, spiritual disciplines, use of time, etc. The man's lifestyle ought to reflect intentional thinking and living, prudence, and wisdom.

3.3.5 "Respectable" (1 Tim. 3:2), "well thought of by outsiders, so that he may not fall into disgrace, into a snare of the devil" (1 Tim. 3:7), and "upright" (Titus 1:8).

These terms represent the outward sense that others have of the elder. He is a man others would describe as "respectable," which means worthy of respect. He is dignified and proper in this outward sense. Yet 1 Timothy 3:7 also warns us that his reputation with those *outside the church* is important as well. The idea here is that if even an unbeliever thinks poorly of the man, how could we possibly elevate him in the church? This is speaking to his character, of course. If his reputation is poor specifically because of his stand for Christ and the gospel or because of slander, that is different. What is in view here is his integrity. It will be a "disgrace" to appoint a man to this office whom even unbelievers think a poor example.

3.3.6 "Hospitable" (1 Tim. 3:2; Titus 1:8)

The "hospitality" required of all Christians (1 Pet. 4:9) is to be practiced by the elder. In his life, there is a general openness to other people, whether demonstrated by shared meals, giving of his time, or simply being consistent in building relationships with others.

3.3.7 "Not a drunkard" (1 Tim. 3:3; Titus 1:7)

The self-mastery of previous characteristics makes it clear that an elder should not be mastered by wine, drugs, or any other substance, but Paul makes it explicit here. Other potentially "addictive" types of activities such as gambling, pornography, computer gaming, or any activity that has overflowed its boundaries in the man's life could potentially apply as well.

3.3.8 "Not violent but gentle" (1 Tim. 3:3; Titus 1:7); "Not quarrelsome" (1 Tim. 3:3), not "quick-tempered" (Titus 1:7)

An elder faces difficult people and difficult situations and faces emotional conflicts between godly people. Thus, a man prone to bully, fight, or be generally "hot-headed" should not serve in this office. An elder must be "correcting his opponents with gentleness" (2 Tim. 2:25) and must "be patient with them all" (1 Thess. 5:14). There is a general ability to bring "peace" to situations of conflict ("peaceable," 1 Tim. 3:3, NASB). Occasional expressions of anger or impatience are simply part of our fallenness, but if these characterize the man for those who live with him—his family, co-workers, others in church—the man must not be an elder.

3.3.9 "Not a lover of money" (1 Tim. 3:3) or "greedy for gain" (Titus 1:7)

There are different ways to be disqualified because a man is a "lover of money." It can mean a general greed that motivates someone to exploit the church for his own financial gain (Titus 1:7; 1 Pet. 5:2), or worse, to steal from it (Eph. 4:28). It can also mean a "covetousness" in the man's life that is really a form of "idolatry" (Col. 3:5), or it could simply be a continual discontent with what God has provided for him (Phil. 4:10-13; Heb. 13:5). All of these are temptations for everyone, but when they are characteristic of a man, he should not serve as an elder.

3.3.10 "A lover of good" (Titus 1:8)

This term in the Greek (*philagathos*) has to do with the heart of the potential elder. It is more than someone described as "a good man" or one committed to do "good works" (Titus 2:14), though it encompasses these. Beneath these is also to be a real love of and commitment to "the good" or "God's best." There is a demonstrated motivation to work for the good in others, in situations, and in his own life. "An overseer's love for people is always to be correlated with a love for what God wants people to be."[4]

3.4 Skilled Managers of Their Homes

Overseers must be skilled managers of their homes with evident fruit in their children. Few qualifications for the elder are as sobering as this one, but none are more telling of the kind of leader that a man will be in God's church. The daily interaction, myriad of situations, unpredictability, balance of love and strength, demand for wisdom, and sheer test of character that happen in a home mirror profoundly the kind of labors an elder is called to in the church. Further, a man

---

[4] George W. Knight III, *The Pastoral Epistles: A Commentary on the Greek Text* (Grand Rapids, Mich.: Eerdmans, 1992) 292.

may keep his true self fairly hidden from his co-workers, but what he truly is will be revealed in his family life.

Yet, while a man's wife and children are a vital evidence of a man's leadership, they are not an infallible one. The heart of the child plays a part in the overall fruitfulness of his or her life. Thus, as we examine a man's household, we must not make hasty judgments.

1 Timothy 3:4-5 and Titus 1:6 spell out the kind of leader in the home that the overseer is to be.

3.4.1 The man must lead his household "well."

The New Testament says of the elder that "he must manage his own household well, with all dignity" (1 Tim. 3:4). The key word used in Timothy is "manage," a term that means "to lead, rule, direct." How a man cares for his house and property and how he leads his wife and children should be included in this requirement.

The passage requires that the man lead his family "well"; all men are the heads of their homes, but we are looking for the man who leads "well." A household kept in order by coercion and threat is clearly inconsistent with the other character traits listed of elders. A potential elder is instead to "manage" his household "with all dignity."

Further, a man who manages his household well is obedient to the commandments related to his role as a father and husband: he is a husband who loves his wife as Christ loved the church (Eph. 5:25-33), he is living with her in an understanding way (1 Pet. 3:7), and he is a father who is bringing his children up in the discipline and instruction of the Lord (Eph. 6:4). In other words, there is a pattern of loving discipleship and gracious leadership in his management of the home.

3.4.2 The character of the children must be evident in their response to the father and their overall behavior (1 Tim. 3:5; Titus 1:6).

A chief evidence of the man's parenting is his children. Their character, behavior, and even faith are seen as proper signs of how "well" he is parenting. The first and basic evidence to examine is that his children are "submissive" (1 Tim. 3:4), not "insubordinate" (Titus 1:6). A man whose leadership inspires the honor, respect, and basic obedience of his children has likely led his family "well" and "with all dignity," not through the threat of violence.

Titus 1:6 adds that an elder must have "faithful children not accused of riot or unruly" (KJV; cf. NET).

We believe the requirement here is for a man's children to be "faithful," not that the children be "believing" (ESV, NASB). The word *pista* can be translated in either way with good biblical precedent,[5] but the context in Titus connects "faithful children" to the issues of "debauchery" and "insubordination," and in 1 Timothy 3:4 the parallel Greek phrase calls for children who are "in submission."

It seems then that Paul is referring to the obedience of the child, not their faith. Further, there is the theological issue that we cannot require the regeneration of a child for the father to be qualified. The spiritual state of the child is in the hands of the Lord, not the father, and is determined "before the foundation of the world" (Eph. 1:4). For these reasons, we believe the Bible requires the elder's children to be obedient to him, not that the children be Christians. The requirement also does not apply to grown children, because adults are responsible for their own behavior and are not bound to obey their parents (even though they continue to "honor" them, Ex. 20:12).

This basic obedience in the elder's children certainly does not mean sinlessness, and we ought to be very slow to disqualify a man for a given incident with one or more of his children. The key question is whether the incident reveals the general foolishness of youth or a characteristic and persistent lack of faithfulness in the father.

Lastly, an elder's children must not be "open to the charge of debauchery" (Titus 1:6). "Debauchery" can include drunkenness (cf. Eph 5:18), but the broader sense perhaps fits better here: "reckless abandon, wild living," "loose living." The question in view here is not a single incident of drunkenness or some other reckless act in the child of a potential elder, but a lifestyle that is out of control in a visible and public manner.

3.4.3   The elder's household is relevant because of the connection between parenting and pastoring.

The Bible makes an explicit connection between caring for your family and caring for Christ's church: "For if someone does not know how to manage his own household, how will he care for God's church?" (1 Tim. 3:5).

The implication is that effective leadership in the home requires a set of gifts that eldership in "God's church" also requires. We can think of the combination of strategic thinking and personal relationship; the need to be both strong and gentle; the need to speak God's truth clearly, but in an environment of love and affection; the challenge of accepting someone

---

[5] For "faithful" as a character trait cf. 1 Cor. 1:9; 10:13; Eph. 6:21; Titus 1:9; 3:8; for "believer" as in "possessing faith in Christ," cf. John 20:27; Acts 10:45.

fully for who they are and yet lovingly calling them on to something greater; and more besides. All of these dichotomies come together in the home and in the church. We believe that it is for this reason that God upholds a man's home as a necessary tool for evaluation.

3.5 Aptitude for Sound Doctrine

Elders must also possess an aptitude for sound doctrine, which means they understand and believe it and can teach and defend it. However, since we are appointing elders and not seminary professors, we might call it an aptitude for *applied* sound doctrine. Beyond this, it includes a facility with the biblical text that demonstrates he is "a worker who has no need to be ashamed, rightly handling the word of truth" (2 Tim. 2:15). This aptitude for sound doctrine has four components to it.

3.5.1 First, the elder must understand sound doctrine (2 Tim. 2:15; Titus 1:9).

From Titus 1:9, we can see that the elder must personally understand "the trustworthy word as taught." A man only barely able to grasp the basics of Christianity will likely be unable to lead others in understanding and believing what the New Testament calls "sound doctrine" (1 Tim. 1:10; Titus 1:9; 2:1). Having an aptitude for doctrine would also include indications that the man is a proven student of the Bible (2 Tim. 2:15).

3.5.2 Second, the elder must believe sound doctrine.

This calls attention to the potential elder's personal faith and confidence in orthodox Christian belief. The challenges of the office require that a man "hold firm" (Titus 1:9) to his own faith if he is going to be able to shepherd people wrestling with theirs.

3.5.3 Third, the pastor must be able to teach sound doctrine (Eph. 4:11; 1 Tim. 3:2; 2 Tim. 3:16-4:2; Titus 1:9).

In 1 Timothy Paul says that the elder must be "able to teach" (3:2), but in Titus we get a sense of the purpose of this aptitude. It is "so that he may be able to give instruction in sound doctrine" (1:9). The teaching he received and believes, he is thus to pass along to others. Such an ability to teach implies a basic ability to organize ideas, accurately exegete the biblical text, and communicate this in a way that encourages, instructs, and even inspires other believers.

3.5.4 Fourth, the pastor must be able to defend sound doctrine (Acts 20:28-30; Titus 1:9).

The final component of the elder's aptitude in sound doctrine brings the first three together: *He must be able to defend sound doctrine to those who challenge or contradict it.* Paul expresses this in Titus 1:9: "He must hold firm to the trustworthy word as taught, so that he may be able to give instruction in sound doctrine and also to rebuke those who contradict it."

Throughout the pastoral epistles, we learn of an array of opponents of the gospel (e.g., 1 Tim. 1:3-7; 2 Tim. 2:14-19; Titus 1:10-16), and throughout the New Testament, we see that the gospel is always being attacked (e.g., Phil. 3:1-12; 2 Pet. 2:1-22). This ability to defend the gospel against its opponents is part of the shepherd's (pastor's) role in guarding the flock entrusted to him from "fierce wolves" both inside and outside the church (Acts 20:28-30).

The skills involved here include (1) discerning the theological issue in question; (2) understanding the truth to combat the lie; and (3) communicating God's truth graciously, which is to find the right word for the moment (Eph. 4:29), or at least a reasonable one. A man cannot be expected to defend all doctrines equally well, but he needs to demonstrate facility with the central doctrines of the church.

This aptitude will likely grow as the man performs the duties of an elder, but to be qualified for ordination to the office, there must be some basic ability to do this. The oral exam of the ordination process, conversation about theological topics, and asking a man how he would respond to hypothetical situations all shed light on a man's ability here.

3.6 The Gift of Leadership

We noted above that the elder is an "overseer" in God's church, leading, managing, and governing the local church according to the revelation of Scripture and Christian prudence, all for the good of the members of the church and the glory of God.

The elder's *responsibility to lead* means that he must possess the necessary *gifting to lead*. This gifting includes having sufficient wisdom to make good decisions in small and large matters, the ability to communicate and implement those decisions, and biblical wisdom to speak into the affairs of the church.

The elder's leadership will involve thinking theologically about the needs of the church and the future direction of the church. Leadership involves a certain amount of casting vision to the church or a segment of the church. A given elder will likely have more gifting in certain areas of the life of the church than in others, but there must be a basic level of leadership to serve as an elder.

There are three places to look when determining a man's fitness to lead in God's church. The first is the most critical: his family (1 Tim. 3:4-5). The second is his current service in the church. How has he demonstrated responsibility, initiative, care, a command of the Scriptures, and a zeal for God in his volunteer work for the church? A third area is his personal and professional life. Is he self-controlled? Conscientious? Able to handle delegated responsibility? Does he have a well-managed life? Such questions can be helpful when ascertaining a man's leadership gift.

3.7 Qualification of an Elder Versus Basis for Removal of an Elder

1 Timothy 3:1-7 and Titus 1:5-9 are given to help us know what to look for in elder candidates in the church. These passages also present the gifting and character traits that called men should continue to cultivate in ministry. The description in these passages should not be viewed as a rigid standard that acts as some trigger to automatically and immediately disqualify a man should he be seen to fall short. If a pastor is found to no longer fit the description in the text, the local elders should explore the situation to determine the reason this is the case.

There is an important difference between the selection process and the removal process for elders. Each church should have a clear process in place to handle the care, evaluation, discipline, and removal of elders. 1 Timothy 5:19-21 is given to help guide us in how to handle an elder who has committed scandalous sin or persists in serious sin for which a public rebuke might be necessary. The proper approach for addressing charges against an elder are addressed in chapter 24 of *The Book of Church Order*.

4 The Elder as Christian *First*

It is critical for both the church and its elders that leadership is seen in a proper light. Pastors and churches suffer when pastors are seen in an inflated manner or as some "professional" class of Christians far removed from "the rest of us." Here are several ideas that should inform a church's view of its elders and the elder's view of himself.

4.1 Overseers are <u>men under authority</u> before they are men entrusted with authority (1 Cor. 11:3, Rom. 1:1).

4.2 Elders are <u>"brothers in Christ"</u> with all those in their church before they are "fathers in the faith" to anyone (Romans 12:10, John 1:12).

4.3 Pastors are also <u>sheep</u> before they are shepherds (John 10:1-15; 1 Pet. 5:4).

4.4 Overseers are <u>servants</u> before they are "leaders" (Heb. 13:17, 1 Tim. 3:4-5).

Elders must see themselves as <u>only one part of the body of Christ</u> with Christ alone as the head (Eph. 1:23; 4:15-16; 5:23; Col. 1:18; 2:19).

5 Elders and Plurality

Elders are to serve as a plurality, not alone; though how many elders constitute adequate plurality is not given in the New Testament. It teaches this by *precedent*, which we see in the fact that all mentions of "elder" are in the plural (e.g., Acts 14:23; 15:2-16:4; Phil. 1:1; 1 Tim. 4:14; etc.).

Plurality is a means of acknowledging that God gives a diversity of gifts to his people (1 Cor. 12:7-11). No one man has all the gifts necessary to lead a local church. While all elders must be "able to teach" (1 Tim. 3:2), some will be more gifted than others. While all of them must have leadership to "manage the household of God" (1 Tim. 3:4), some will have gifting along administrative lines and others along more strategic lines.

Plurality will often mean that different elders will have different responsibilities in the church that line up with their gifting as much as is feasible. Further, when decisions are made in the life of the church, often one man possesses more wisdom in a given area than the others. At such times, there is a kind of mutual deference that is most prudent. Even the role of senior pastor or lead elder is merely an extension of this principle (see BCO-7).

Plurality is one of the key means by which elders are held accountable in an ongoing manner. A man who ministers alone is in a precarious position, able to lean on his own understanding too much, and potentially able to walk in secret sins for a length of time. Plurality does not eliminate these dangers, but it does make them less tempting in the normal flow of life.

It is possible that a church plant will have a season in which only one elder is ordained. The New Testament certainly can envision an authentic church without a plurality of elders (e.g., the period of time prior to Acts 14:23). However, we see this as a temporary necessity that is to be remedied as quickly as possible (without making the opposite error of "laying hands on too quickly"). One remedy is for the sending church elders or the Regional Leader to serve as a functional part of the local eldership until a qualified elder is raised up and ordained. An additional important point is that the second elder, once ordained, need not be full time or financially compensated, at least in the short run.

The precedent of a plurality in the New Testament cannot be an excuse to overlook the requirements of the man who is to be an elder. These are too clear to be overlooked or minimized, and a church will likely suffer more from elders who are unqualified men than it will from having too few elders in office.

6 Bi-Vocational Elders

Elders needn't serve full-time nor be paid staff to be considered true elders. Although they must meet biblical qualifications, they do not need to be seminary or Pastors College graduates. They may serve part-time with or without pay. Although we call such elders bi-vocational elders (the term "lay elders" is also used) as a convenient way to distinguish them from full-time elders, this in no way communicates a diminished role or importance in the church. The Bible allows us to ordain part-time elders or those who will be unpaid for their service. Christian prudence, the needs of the church, the lack of finances, as well as a desire to achieve plurality with well-qualified elders who are already vocationally employed in other roles are some viable reasons to employ bi-vocational elders.

As desirable as this role may be for the health and mission of the church, we should aspire for elders to be paid commensurate to their workload when possible (1 Cor. 9:6-14; Luke 10:7/Matt. 10:10; Gal. 6:6; 1 Tim. 5:17-18). The New Testament teaches that this is so elders can be free to devote themselves to their ministries. 1 Timothy 5:17-18 makes this clear:

> *Let the elders who rule well be considered worthy of double honor, especially those who labor in preaching and teaching.* ¹⁸*For the Scripture says, "You shall not muzzle an ox when it treads out the grain," and, "the laborer deserves his wages."*

Paul's first point here has to do with the relative levels of gifting ("rule well"), scopes of responsibility ("especially those who labor in preaching and teaching"), and apparently financial compensation ("double honor") of elders in a given church. That they are paid seems assumed by the mention of "double honor," and especially by the next verse about "the laborer" deserving his "wages."

His second point is about the need to compensate the elder financially. He is the "ox" who should not be "muzzled" by refusing to compensate him; he is the "laborer" who "deserves his wages" (v. 18). To fail to support him financially can limit his ability and is thus "muzzling the ox." That is a bad thing according to Paul, for it means appointing him to do the work and then hindering him from doing it.

Of course, a church may be unable to fully financially support a pastor for a time. There is nothing that forbids an elder working another job. Additionally, serving bi-vocationally may best serve the needs and mission of the local church depending on the particular elder, his gifting, life-situation, and availability to serve full time. Viable alternatives to full-time pay include providing stipends for preaching and teaching, covering a book allowance, or paying at a part-time level. In some cases, a pastor may simply enjoy being able to serve free of charge. However, if this is not the case and the church is financially able to remunerate him, then the elders should give due consideration to the biblical onus to "not muzzle the ox" and consider financial compensation.

As helpful, wise, and fitting as it may be to employ bi-vocational elders with alternative pay arrangements, there is no clear biblical warrant to withhold pay from an elder merely to create a certain number of unpaid elders for the sake of balancing the amount of paid elders.

Some have believed this provides accountability for paid elders who may experience a conflict of interest due to receiving compensation from the church they serve. While the concept of a balance of power is a good thing when it comes to civil government, the Scriptures never teach that a special category of unpaid or "lay" elders should be appointed for the purpose of "balancing" the power of the paid elders. A biblical answer to such a need is a plurality of elders. In Sovereign Grace, we also benefit from the role of the Regional Assembly of Elders and a Regional Leader, who provide further accountability to such pluralities. Additionally, a healthy relationship with the entire church along with their responsibility to follow biblical judicial proceedings for errant elders provide further accountability.

Given all these considerations, utilizing qualified and gifted bi-vocational elders as full-fledged participants in a church's eldership can be a very effective way to serve the care and mission of the local church and this union of churches.

7 The Senior Pastor

7.1 Use of the Terms "Lead Pastor," "Lead Elder," or "Senior Pastor"

The role of "senior pastor" or "lead pastor/elder" is supportable by biblical precedent and practical wisdom. It is not a biblical office *per se* and therefore not absolutely required in this polity. Nonetheless, the Bible presents numerous examples of groups in the Bible where a man is or becomes the leader, or at least the spokesman. Whether it is Moses over Israel, heads of tribes and clans in Israel, judges and kings over Israel, Peter over the Twelve apostles, or James in the Jerusalem church, it seems that biblically there is typically a man identified as the leader or spokesman (e.g., Acts 1:15; 15:13ff.). Further, practical wisdom tells us that a group is served when one individual is identified as the primary leader or spokesman, even if he is technically a "first among equals." He is an equal among his fellow elders in the exercise of authority, not another class of elder, but his role is distinct in that he serves as a leader of his fellow elders.

The lead elder is part of a plurality of elders, and his character and gifting are not necessarily uniformly greater than that of the other men. What is distinct is his measure of gifting and capacity in those areas (teaching, leadership) most central to pastoral leadership. The precise nature of the role of the lead pastor may vary depending on the maturity of an eldership, the range of gifts on the team, the level of specialization on the team, etc. The elders decide who will serve in this capacity (with appropriate input from church members and guiding counsel from other leaders in Sovereign Grace).

Sovereign Grace churches have historically and wisely delegated some of the following responsibilities to senior pastors.

- Providing doctrinal leadership through a prominent teaching role
- Developing the eldership into a cohesive leadership team
- Providing pastoral care for the eldership
- Facilitating decision-making by serving as Chairman of the Board of local elders
- Identifying and deploying spiritual gifts among the elders
- Encouraging efficiency
- Coordinating eldership training
- Acting as spokesman for the elders

7.2 Procedure for the Repositioning of the Senior Pastor

7.2.1 General Principles

7.2.1.1
Although we affirm both the biblical principles underlying a first among equals and the wisdom of having such a role among the elders of a church, the Senior Pastorate is not a biblical office as such; therefore, the Scriptures do not give us

either qualifications or procedures for the installation or repositioning of a Senior Pastor.

7.2.1.2 The title of a Senior Pastor (Lead Elder, Lead Pastor) expresses the recognition that though all elders are equal in responsibilities and authority, they are not necessarily equal in gifting, especially in the gift of leadership.

7.2.1.3 It is often the elder who is the most gifted preacher and leader that is identified as the Senior Pastor.

7.2.1.4 It is ultimately the responsibility of the eldership of a local church to identify and commission each of its members to fulfill tasks and responsibilities as they see fit, including the Senior Pastorate (see BCO-7.1).

7.2.1.5 Because of the visibility that a Senior Pastor has, and because of the unique and important role in which he serves with respect to the congregation, repositioning him should be done carefully and according to the procedure outlined below.

The following steps are given in an attempt to best protect the Senior Pastor's church, his eldership, and his ministry:

7.2.2 Procedure

7.2.2.1 If some of the elders think the eldership needs to consider the question of repositioning the Senior Pastor (for reasons other than moral qualifications or heterodoxy), then the matter should be brought to all of the local elders for the purpose of making an evaluation.

7.2.2.2 The concerns of the questioning elder(s) should be honestly and clearly spoken and communicated to the entire eldership. Once the eldership agrees that an evaluation is needed, but before any decision has been made, the elders should send a communication to the Regional Leader that outlines their observations and the reason(s) for evaluation of the Senior Pastor. This formalizes the process of the Senior Pastor evaluation.

7.2.2.3 A clearly defined formal plan of evaluation should be established by the local eldership including:

7.2.2.3.a A clear presentation of the issues precipitating such an evaluation.

7.2.2.3.b An opportunity for the Senior Pastor to respond to his fellow elders.

7.2.2.3.c A suitable period of time (at least 30 days) for evaluation of the Senior Pastor in light of the needs of the congregation in order to determine if the elder(s)' concerns are legitimate. If applicable, the

Senior Pastor should be given time for improvement in areas of concern.

    7.2.2.3.d   The seeking of input and advice from elders in the region and the Regional Leader.

    7.2.2.3.e   A suitable means of getting input from other local leaders and those within the congregation.

7.2.2.4   A copy of the plan should be sent to the Regional Leader.

7.2.2.5   At the end of the evaluation period, the elders will make their decision based upon the due consideration of the gifts and abilities of the Senior Pastor, his abilities relative to the other elders, and a proper assessment of the needs of the local congregation. While the elders may seek advice from the Regional Leader and other Sovereign Grace elders, the decision ultimately rests with the local elders.

7.2.2.6   The local eldership will communicate in writing their decision to the Regional Leader who will inform the Regional Assembly of Elders.

7.2.2.7   If the decision to reposition the Senior Pastor is made, the one being repositioned has the right to resign with honor if he decides not to remain on the eldership. The Regional Leader and the Sovereign Grace Director of Church Development will facilitate, when possible, his transition to another Sovereign Grace church if he so desires. Sovereign Grace is under no obligation to ensure his placement on another church's staff or eldership but will make an effort to do so. The church that repositioned the Senior Pastor should make every effort to give appropriate considerations to the departing pastor including severance.

7.2.3 Subsequent Appeals

7.2.3.1   If the Senior Pastor believes the local eldership sinned against him, he will have the right to appeal to the Regional Judicial Review Committee.

7.2.3.2   If the Senior Pastor believes the elders did not follow the procedure outlined above, he has the right to appeal to the Regional Judicial Review Committee.

7.2.3.3   If the Judicial Review Committee finds in favor of the eldership, no other appeal will be granted.

7.2.3.4   If the Judicial Review Committee finds in favor of the removed Senior Pastor, it may appeal to the eldership to re-do the evaluation, but it does not have the authority to force his reinstatement.

7.2.4 Final Disposition

7.2.4.1 A Senior Pastor or other elder who is <u>repositioned,</u> not on the basis of moral qualification or heterodoxy, and chooses to leave the local church leaves with honor, remains in good standing within Sovereign Grace, and thus retains his ordination status.

7.2.4.2 A Senior Pastor, or any other elder who is <u>removed</u> from office, but not on the basis of moral disqualification or heterodoxy, remains in good standing within Sovereign Grace and retains his ordination status.

8 Accountability for Pastors

Because significant authority is entrusted to elders, it is critical that these men are accountable. They are accountable in several ways.

8.1 Accountability to God First

First and most importantly, elders are appointed to their office ultimately by God: "The Holy Spirit has made you overseers" (Acts 20:28). This means that they must perform their office with a keen awareness of God's watchful eye on them: "I charge you in the presence of God and of Christ Jesus, who is to judge the living and the dead, and by his appearing and his kingdom: preach the word" (2 Tim. 4:1-2a). Further, they are to perform their duties now in light of a coming judgment: "When the chief Shepherd appears, you will receive the unfading crown of glory" (1 Pet. 5:4).

8.2 The Ordination Process

There is also accountability in the ordination process. While there is no immunity to sin or temptation this side of our glorification, we do a great service to the church when we refuse to appoint anyone to this office who does not explicitly fulfill all the prerequisites given in the New Testament. This is a preemptive measure, but an important one. If we are careless about whom we ordain to the office in the first place, any accountability structures we implement will be of limited value.

8.3 Plurality of Elders

If a church has faithfully appointed a plurality of elders to the office, there is a great accountability that occurs. Some of this accountability will happen through formal, scheduled times of speaking into each other's lives; asking about specific areas of obedience must be a part of a healthy plurality. Accountability also happens in the ongoing flow of ministry as sinful patterns emerge in a man's leadership or lifestyle or in isolated incidents that occur before others. A healthy awareness of each other's behavior and an expectation of input and observations from others will supplement the formal accountability in a helpful way. Truly, to serve in a plurality of elders involves a commitment to ongoing accountability.

8.4 The Congregation

There is a critical layer of accountability that comes from the congregation when it brings observations and appeals to elders or charges against elders. Just as the man to be qualified as an elder must have a general openness to input, so must the elder remain open to the observations of those in the church. "Fools despise wisdom and instruction" (Prov. 1:7). At times an elder might even be engaged in a matter of personal sin against another person in the church, one that requires a Matthew 18:15-20 process of rebuke, repentance, and reconciliation.

A critical point of accountability is what Paul labels "a charge against an elder" (1 Tim. 5:19). He is not specific about whether this accusation comes from an apostle or a member of the congregation or another elder, but we should probably assume that all three are possibilities.

A member of a congregation must be enabled to pursue such accusations against leaders. Without this layer of accountability, the possibility of some version of tyrannical leadership is easy to imagine. Further, denying such due process to the congregation opens us up to a situation where a person could observe an elder failing in his office and be unable to act on it. Of course, the right to do this does not mean that they can do this without any restraints (Cf. BCO-24).

8.5 Sovereign Grace

In all of the ways specified in this *Book of Church Order*, elders in a local church are accountable to the other elders in their Region and ultimately to all the elders in Sovereign Grace. Regional Assemblies with their Judicial Review Committees and the Council of Elders, along with the Sovereign Grace Court of Appeal, provide accountability for the life and doctrine of elders in Sovereign Grace.

9 The Ordination of Elders

9.1 Introduction

Ordination in Sovereign Grace churches is that act by which men are set apart to the office of elder (Acts 14:23). It is the church's solemn approval of and public attestation to a man's inward call, his gifts, and his appointment to pastoral ministry. Before a man is ordained to the office of elder he has been first called, gifted, and chosen through divine initiative (Acts 20:28, Eph. 4:11). In Sovereign Grace appointing a man to the office of elder involves a collaborative effort between the elders and members of a local church and the Regional Assembly of Elders.

The purpose of a process for ordination is simply to appoint men to this office who resemble the New Testament criteria for the office (especially 1 Tim. 3:1-7; Titus 1:5-9). We are not omniscient and do not know the future, but a process helps us not to miss obvious deficiencies in a man who desires this office.

A man ordained by a Sovereign Grace church retains his ordination status in Sovereign Grace unless the Regional Assembly of Elders revokes his status as a result of discipline or significant exception to the Statement of Faith or explicitly mandated practices in the Book of Church Order. An ordained man not currently serving as an elder may perform sacerdotal duties with the approval of an elder in a Sovereign Grace church.

9.2 Feedback throughout the process

During the ordination process, members of the candidate's church are given opportunity to submit in writing their observations, affirmation, or critique of the man in question. This is not to propagate gossip and slander but to allow opportunity to stop the process if there is information the elders lack in evaluating the man. Additionally, affirmation will help confirm the selection of the candidate. Such feedback is an important opportunity for the congregation to assist in the ordination process.

The feedback of members of the candidate's church will not be understood as a binding vote on the ordination of the candidate but may be a deciding factor in his qualification. It will be up to the local eldership to handle the feedback as they deem most appropriate.

The candidate's church may decide to utilize some or all of the following practices to help ensure full participation of the congregation in this very important decision.

- Teaching the congregation about the biblical basis for their affirmation in this process and the sobriety of the task;
- Making a formal announcement of the candidacy of the potential elder to the congregation at the beginning of the ordination process;

- Announcing the qualifications and charging the church to soberly consider their role in affirmation;
- Issuing a written form for official feedback;
- Soliciting personal letters or other written feedback from congregants;
- Obtaining formal written feedback from all members;
- Arranging personal interviews with congregants to discuss their feedback and solicit further input if necessary;
- Publicizing the results of the affirmation of the congregation;
- Announcing the close of the affirmation process ahead of time;
- Preparing the church for their vows of affirmation of the candidate during the ordination service.

9.3 The Basic Process for Ordination

Each church eldership has the responsibility and authority to select, test, and ordain future elders in a manner of their choosing. What follows is a recommended, but not mandated, process. What is required is that each elder successfully complete the Sovereign Grace ordination requirements, including subscribing to the *Sovereign Grace Statement of Faith* and pledging to adhere to the stipulated rules of the *Sovereign Grace Book of Church Order*. Once the Regional Assembly approves the elder candidate, the local church then ordains and installs the elder.

9.3.1 The elders decide to choose a man who is qualified as much as they can determine.

The local eldership bears primary responsibility for examining the life and doctrine of candidates for pastoral ministry in order to determine whether the candidate meets the biblical character qualifications (cf. BCO-3) and fully agrees with the Sovereign Grace *Statement of Faith* (cf. BCO-9.3.6 below). Elders will solicit input from those who know the man and pay close attention to his current service. Such indicators are not infallible, but they do help establish the man's fitness for pastoral ministry. Appropriate counsel may be sought from the Sovereign Grace Regional Leader or other elders in the region.

9.3.2 Input from all church officers and congregants.

In this initial stage of evaluation, input will be solicited from the elders, deacons, and congregation on an ad hoc basis. The elders will together establish if the man is qualified as far as can be seen.

9.3.3 The congregation is informed and input is invited.

Once the elders are supportive of the man for pastoral ministry, they will notify the church and invite their further input.

While it is primarily the elders of the local church who select and test candidates for pastoral ministry, the Regional Assembly of Elders, its

Ordination Committee, and the congregation also have a vital role in the ordination process. In order for some elder qualifications to be determined, congregational input is important.

Even though Titus was given the singular charge of appointing elders in Crete (Titus 1:5), the appointment process of potential overseers would seem to require the testimony of other believers in order to determine who was blameless and above reproach, hospitable, not pugnacious, not greedy for gain, whose children were not open to the charge of debauchery, etc. (Titus 1:5-9). Further, attestation to many of these leadership qualifications seems to require proof over a period of time by a local church (1 Tim. 3:10).

Therefore, the active involvement of the congregation is vital in the confirmation of an elder's call and, at a minimum, should require extensive informal interaction with the congregation regarding the suitability of the elder candidate.

9.3.4 Pastors College

Candidates for the office of elder preferably will attend the Sovereign Grace Pastors College or a functional equivalent. However, this is not an absolute requirement, and candidates will only be required to meet standards set by the local church along with passing the requirements for ordination under the agency of the Regional Assembly of Elders as specified herein.

9.3.5 Pastoral Internship

Prior to ordination candidates should ideally serve as pastoral interns. The length and nature of this internship will be decided by the local eldership.

9.3.6 Successful Completion of Sovereign Grace ordination requirements

9.3.6.1 Only the eldership of a local church can ordain new elders (BCO-1.3). Therefore, the local eldership bears primary responsibility for selecting candidates for pastoral ministry and examining their life and doctrine in order to determine whether the candidate meets the biblical character qualifications (BCO-3) and fully agrees with the Sovereign Grace *Statement of Faith*.

However, since the quality and unity of our elders is fundamental to the nature and health of our union, a common commitment to the standards for elders necessitates that all elders in Sovereign Grace churches be approved according to the standards of this *Book of Church Order* through the agency of the Regional Assembly of Elders (BCO-1.9). Ordination and discipline of an elder in any Sovereign Grace church is valid in and recognized by all other Sovereign Grace churches.

9.3.6.2 The pastoral candidate must complete all of the Sovereign Grace requirements for ordination before his actual ordination. These include (1) completing all work required in the current Sovereign Grace ordination standards, (2) passing the written and oral ordination exams administered by the Regional Ordination Committee, and (3) and approval by a simple majority of the Regional Assembly of Elders, after any necessary and relevant questioning. Certain of these aspects are further defined below.

9.3.6.3 After the candidate has passed the ordination exams, he must affirm in writing the statement below. The candidate will sign two copies of this statement and make two additional photocopies (one signed statement kept by candidate and one sent to Sovereign Grace; one photocopy given to Regional Ordination Committee and one to the Director of Church Development):

"I declare sincerely before God that I believe that all the articles and points of doctrine contained in the Sovereign Grace Statement of Faith fully agree with the Scriptures, and I own that Statement as the statement and confession of my faith. These are doctrines I promise to teach and defend in public and in private. I promise further that if in the future I come to have reservations about any of these doctrines, I will share these reservations with my eldership and the Regional Assembly of Elders.

If ordained, I will submit to the explicitly mandated polity practices of the Sovereign Grace Book of Church Order. I affirm that the form of government contained in the Sovereign Grace Book of Church Order is a wise and suitable application of Scriptural principles."

If the candidate has any reservations about or takes any exception to either the *Statement of Faith* or the explicitly mandated practices of *The Book of Church Order*, he must inform his local eldership and the Regional Assembly of Elders. These exceptions must be submitted in writing, and each elder's exceptions shall be kept on record with the local eldership, the Regional Assembly of Elders, and Sovereign Grace.

The local eldership shall first investigate the exception before presenting the candidate to the Regional Assembly of Elders. If required, the Regional Assembly of Elders shall then determine the significance of the candidate's exceptions. If the exception is trivial or semantic and not a substantive difference with any doctrine in the *Statement of Faith* or explicitly mandated practices in *The Book of Church Order*, then the candidate may sign the above statements and be put forward for a vote on his ordination. However, if it is determined that the candidate substantially disagrees with any of the doctrines of the *Statement of Faith* or any explicitly mandated practices of *The Book of Church Order*, he may not be approved for ordination. The Ordination Committee shall recommend to him a course of study on the relevant doctrines and principles, if the candidate is willing, in the hopes that his exceptions might be overcome.

9.3.6.4 The above statements having been signed, the candidate will then be presented to the Regional Assembly for a vote on his ordination. The local eldership shall publicly commend the gifting and character of the candidate. The Regional Ordination Committee shall testify that the candidate has passed all required ordination exams. The Regional Assembly shall then question the candidate as they see fit to validate that there is no heterodoxy or scandalous sin present in the candidate that would prohibit the candidate from being approved for ordination.

9.3.6.5 The Regional Assembly then votes on whether to approve the candidate for ordination. Approval requires a simple majority vote. As stipulated by *The Book of Church Order* (13.2.1.5), the Regional Elders must demonstrate just cause to reject a candidate who has been previously vetted by his local church and has passed the required ordination examinations. Just cause consists exclusively of heterodoxy (i.e., deviation from the Sovereign Grace *Statement of Faith*) or scandalous or serious sin.

9.3.6.6 The above steps having been completed, the candidate is now ready to be ordained by his local church eldership.

9.3.7 Date Set for Ordination

Once the man is established as qualified for this office and the church desires to appoint him to this office, a date is set for the ordination service and is announced to the church.

9.3.8   Final Written Feedback

Written feedback is allowable throughout the evaluation and ordination process but should be finalized at least 30 days in advance of the ordination service.

9.3.9   The Ordination Service

Local church elders will be present at the ordination service. Further, whenever possible, the Regional Leader or his representative will also be present to commend the candidate.

During the ordination service, the presiding elder(s) will include the following questions for the candidate to answer in the affirmative:

- *Do you promise to shepherd the flock of God not under compulsion but willingly, not for shameful gain but eagerly, not domineering over those in your charge but being an example to the flock? (1 Pet. 5:1-4)*

- *Do you promise to faithfully guard the flock over which the Holy Spirit has made you an overseer, and do you promise to protect that flock from false teaching, division, and dissension? (Acts 20:28-31)*

- *Do you promise to care for the flock of God, not as a hireling, but as an under shepherd of the Great Shepherd, caring for his sheep as the precious ones for whom he died? (Ezek. 34)*

- *Do you, in the presence of God and of Christ Jesus and this congregation, promise to preach the Word in season and out of season, and do you promise to reprove, rebuke, and exhort with complete patience, enduring suffering, while remaining sober-minded in all of your preaching and teaching, and will you do the work of an evangelist among those whom God has given you charge? (2 Tim. 4:1-5)*

- *Do you declare sincerely before God that you believe all the articles and points of doctrine contained in the Sovereign Grace Statement of Faith fully agree with the Scriptures? Do you own that Statement as the statement and confession of your faith? And do you promise to teach and defend these doctrines in public and private?*

- *Do you promise further that if in the future you come to have reservations about any of these doctrines, you will share these reservations with your eldership and the Regional Assembly of Elders?*

- *Do you promise to keep a close watch on yourself and to walk humbly before others, to be self-suspicious of your own motives, to invite*

- *criticism from others, and to make yourself accountable to those whom God has put in your life?*

- *Do you submit without exception to the explicitly mandated practices of the Sovereign Grace Book of Church Order, affirming that that form of government is a wise and suitable application of Scriptural principles?*

- *Do you promise to walk in a manner worthy of the gospel and to show yourself in all respects, in action and in speech, to be a model of good works, integrity, and dignity so that neither the church, nor our Savior Jesus Christ, nor the gospel may be brought into reproach? (Titus 2:7-8)*

- *Do you promise to continually seek the gifts of the Spirit that you might serve God's people, not in the energy of the flesh, but in the power of the Holy Spirit and to carry out your ministry without fear of man?*

The candidate having answered in the affirmative, the presiding elder will ask the church the following, expecting an affirmative reply:

- *Do you, the people of _____ church, receive _____ as your pastor?*

- *Do you promise to receive the word of truth from him with meekness and love and to submit to him in the due biblical exercise of his leadership?*

- *Do you promise to supply him with whatever material support he may need to fulfill his ministry among you?*

- *Do you promise to encourage him in his labors and to assist his ministry and leadership for your spiritual edification, the evangelization of the lost, and the promotion of God's glory?*

All the local elders and the Regional Leader will lay hands on the candidate and pray for him. The process of "laying on of hands" is a public affirmation and recognition that this individual has been set apart for gospel ministry, and that the ongoing mercy and attendance of the Spirit of God will be necessary to satisfactorily fulfill the requirements of ministry.

9.4 The Duration of the Office of Overseer

It is assumed that when a man is ordained to this office, he will serve as long as he is qualified and it is in the best interest of the church and his family. In other words, there is no set term on an elder's service. Term limits seem to be a contradiction to the way that God gifts his people and the example he gives us in the New Testament.

9.5 Churches without Elders

As an expression of our unity and commitment to mutual care, if a local church is without any elders (e.g., because it has only been recently adopted, or because all of its elders have resigned, been disavowed, or died), the responsibilities and authority of the local eldership shall devolve upon the Regional Assembly of Elders. Under the coordinating direction of the Regional Leader, the members of the Regional Assembly shall supply the pulpit and fulfill the church's pastoral needs. In close consultation with the congregation (in accordance with BCO-9.2 and BCO-11), the Regional Assembly will select an elder for the church by a simple majority vote. The Regional Assembly of Elders should honor the church's previous practices concerning the affirmation of elders. At that time, all of the responsibilities and authority of the church's local eldership shall revert from the Regional Assembly back to the elder.

9.6 Taking New Exceptions to the *Statement of Faith* or the explicitly mandated practices of the *Book of Church Order*

Any time that an elder registers new exceptions to the *Statement of Faith* or the explicitly mandated practices of the *Book of Church Order*, he must inform his eldership and the Regional Assembly of Elders. These exceptions must be submitted in writing, and the elder's exceptions shall be kept on record with the local eldership, the Regional Assembly of Elders, and Sovereign Grace.

The local eldership shall first investigate the exception(s) before presenting the elder's exception(s) to the Regional Assembly of Elders. The Regional Assembly of Elders shall then determine the significance of the elder's exception(s). If the Regional Assembly of Elders determines that the exception is trivial or semantic and not substantively different from any doctrine in the *Statement of Faith* or explicitly mandated practices in the *Book of Church Order*, then that decision shall be kept on record with the elder's exceptions. However, if it is determined that the elder substantially disagrees with any of the doctrines of the *Statement of Faith* or any explicitly mandated practices of the *Book of Church Order*, the Ordination Committee shall recommend to him a course of study on the relevant doctrines and principles, if the elder is willing, in the hopes that his exceptions might be overcome.

If the elder's exceptions are not overcome, the Regional Assembly of Elders shall vote to revoke his ordination status by three-fourths vote and determine the timing of the revocation. The elder is thereby removed from the local eldership.

9.7 Transfer of Ordination Status within Sovereign Grace Churches

Ordination and discipline of an elder in any Sovereign Grace church are valid and recognized by all other Sovereign Grace churches. A man previously ordained within Sovereign Grace in good standing who accepts a call to serve at another church need not, therefore, re-take the ordination exam or repeat any other part of the ordination process.

Each church eldership has the responsibility and authority to select and install existing ordained men as elders in a manner of their choosing. Each ordained man must be in good standing (cf. BCO-3), subscribe to the Sovereign Grace Churches' *Statement of Faith*, and pledge to adhere to the explicitly mandated practices of the Sovereign Grace Churches' *Book of Church Order*. If he has any exceptions to either the *Statement of Faith* or the explicitly mandated practices of the *Book of Church Order*, he shall submit them for review to the Regional Assembly of Elders.

9.7.1 The elders review the man's qualifications as much as they can determine.

The local eldership bears primary responsibility for confirming that the life and doctrine of any ordained man they seek to install as an elder continues to meet the biblical character qualifications (cf. BCO-3) and continues to agree with the Sovereign Grace Churches' *Statement of Faith* and the explicitly mandated practices of the *Book of Church Order* (cf. BCO-9.3.6 above). Elders will solicit input from those who know the man and pay special attention to his previous service as an elder. Appropriate counsel may be sought from the Sovereign Grace Regional Leader(s), Regional Ordination Committee(s) and other elders across the region(s).

The ordained man must reaffirm in writing the statement in BCO-9.3.6.3. If the man has any reservations with or takes exception to the *Statement of Faith* or the explicitly mandated practices of the *Book of Church Order*, he must inform the eldership calling him and their Regional Assembly of Elders. The eldership receiving him shall first investigate the exception before presenting the ordained man to the Regional Assembly of Elders. These exceptions must be submitted in writing, and each elder's exceptions shall be kept on record with the eldership receiving him, their Regional Assembly of Elders, and Sovereign Grace.

9.7.2 Possible interview by the Regional Assembly of Elders

If the ordained man is not a current member of the Regional Assembly of Elders or if he is registering a new exception to either the *Statement of Faith* or the explicitly mandated practices of the *Book of Church Order*, the Regional Ordination Committee must interview him, inquire about any exceptions and make a recommendation to the Regional Assembly of Elders about whether these are trivial or semantic exceptions acceptable among elders or substantive differences that warrant a rejection of the ordination transfer.

9.7.3 The congregation is informed and their input is invited.

Once the elders are supportive of installing the ordained man for pastoral ministry, they will notify the congregation as early in the process as practical and involve it appropriately in the process.

9.7.4 Approval by the Regional Assembly of Elders

If the ordained man is not a current member of the Regional Assembly of Elders, the local elders will put forth the ordained man to the Regional Assembly of Elders who, with input from the Regional Ordination Committee, will vote to affirm the transfer of his ordination status with a simple majority.

The Regional Assembly may only reject the transfer of ordination because of either heterodoxy (i.e., deviation from the Sovereign Grace *Statement of Faith*), scandalous or serious sin (BCO-9.3.6.5), or significant exception to the explicitly mandated practices of the *Book of Church Order*.

If the ordained man has registered any new exceptions to either the *Statement of Faith* or the explicitly mandated practices of the *Book of Church Order*, the Regional Assembly of Elders shall determine the significance of the man's exceptions. If the exception is trivial or semantic and not substantively different from any doctrine in the *Statement of Faith* or explicitly mandated practices in the *Book of Church Order*, then the man may sign the above statements and be put forward for a vote on the transfer of his ordination status. However, if it is determined that the ordained man substantially disagrees with any of the doctrines of the *Statement of Faith* or explicitly mandated practices in the *Book of Church Order*, his ordination transfer may not be approved. The Ordination Committee shall recommend to him a course of study on the relevant doctrines and principles, if the ordained man is willing, in the hopes that his exceptions might be overcome. If his exceptions are not overcome, the Regional Assembly of Elders shall refer him back to his current eldership to address the new exception(s) as described in BCO-9.6.

9.7.5 The installation service

Once the ordained man is reaffirmed as qualified for office and the church desires to install him as an elder, the installation service may be carried out as described in BCO-9.3.7 and 9.3.9.

9.8 Transfer of Ordination Status Across Denominations

A man ordained as an elder in a denomination other than Sovereign Grace may be eligible to have that ordination transferred into Sovereign Grace. The key questions to answer in evaluating this transfer are (1) how equivalent his ordination is to the Sovereign Grace ordination standards and (2) whether he is qualified according to Sovereign Grace standards. This assessment will involve several regional committees and ultimately the entire Regional Assembly of Elders. It is assumed that the candidate has been linked to a specific region through his involvement with Sovereign Grace.

9.8.1 The Regional Church Planting Committee will use their guidelines and best practices document to conduct a full assessment of the candidate's character and compatibility with our theology, mission, values, and polity (cf. BCO-13.2.5.2). They will submit their assessment and recommendations to the Regional Leader.

9.8.2 The Regional Ordination Committee will assess the doctrine of the candidate elder. The Ordination Committee will make a recommendation to the Regional Assembly of Elders for or against the transfer of each elder's ordination status. The Regional Ordination Committee may recommend to the Regional Assembly of Elders that the elder fulfill the Sovereign Grace Ordination Standards and exams if it judges this prudent.

9.8.3 The elder candidate will sign these two statements as an expression of his commitment to the doctrine and polity of Sovereign Grace:

Affirmation of the Sovereign Grace Statement of Faith

I declare sincerely before God that I believe that all the articles and points of doctrine contained in the Sovereign Grace Statement of Faith fully agree with the Scriptures, and I own that Statement as the statement and confession of my faith. These are doctrines I promise to teach and defend in public and in private. I promise further that if in the future I come to have reservations about any of these doctrines, I will share these reservations with my eldership and the Regional Assembly of Elders.

Submission to the Sovereign Grace Book of Church Order

If ordained I will submit to the explicitly mandated polity practices of the Sovereign Grace Book of Church Order. I affirm that the form of government contained in the Sovereign Grace Book of Church Order is a wise and suitable application of Scriptural principles.

If the elder candidate has any reservations about or takes any exceptions to these two statements, he must communicate these in writing to the Regional Leader and the Regional Assembly of Elders.

These reservations and/or exceptions will be investigated by the Regional Ordination Committee, who will then make a recommendation to the Regional Assembly of Elders about whether these are trivial semantic exceptions acceptable among elders or substantive differences that warrant a rejection of the ordination transfer.

9.8.4 The Regional Assembly of Elders receives from the Regional Leader the relevant reports from the regional committees regarding the elder candidate 30 days prior to taking a vote on the candidate. Once these are received the Regional Assembly can vote on whether to transfer the elder's ordination into Sovereign Grace or not. A vote by simple majority is required to transfer the ordination.

9.8.5 If the Regional Assembly votes in favor of the ordination transfer, the Regional Leader will notify the Executive Director and send a written copy of the affirmation statements in 9.8.3 to the Regional Leader and the Executive Director.

9.8.6 After the vote by the Regional Assembly, the elder may be installed for service in a local church through a service modeled after BCO-9.3.7-9.3.9.

9.9 The Voluntary Resignation of an Elder from Office

Circumstances may arise such that an elder chooses to resign from office willingly, whether confessing to serious sin, acknowledging significant doctrinal disagreement, or for personal reasons.

9.9.1 *Resignation Agreement*: A written *Resignation Agreement* must be created, which defines the terms and conditions of the elder's resignation (e.g., timing, reason, severance). This agreement is between the local elders and the resigning elder. The resigning elder, the local eldership, the Regional Leader, the Chairman of the Regional Judicial Review Committee, and the Sovereign Grace Director of Church Development all must receive a copy of the *Resignation Agreement*.

9.9.2 While this is a local church situation, a Moderator of Just Cause appointed by the Regional Judicial Review Committee must review the matter to determine whether or not the resignation is fair and mutually agreed upon.

9.9.3 The review must be in keeping with the *Rules of Procedure*, addressing the issues found there. The following questions must be answered.

9.9.3.1 Are each party's reasons for the resignation clearly stated in the *Resignation Agreement*?

9.9.3.2 Is there a clear understanding on the part of both parties regarding the implications and conditions of the *Resignation Agreement*?

9.9.3.3 Is the standing of the resigning elder's ordination status clearly stated and agreed upon in the *Resignation Agreement*?

9.9.3.4 Is the *Resignation Agreement* in keeping with the stipulations of the *Book of Church Order*, especially BCO-9 and BCO-24?

10 The Office of Deacon

10.1 Biblical Basis

There are numerous passages in the New Testament that use the Greek term *diakonos* and its cognates (Rom. 16:1, Eph. 6:21, Col. 1:7, Col. 4:7, Phil. 1:1, Acts 6:1-6). The word "deacon" (*diakonos*) simply means "servant" or "minister." In one sense, all God's people are called as "ministers" or "deacons." However, there seems to be an official role for some to share that is designated with the title of "deacon." Although many passages give us a sense that a deacon is a mature servant of the local church, the clearest passage on the qualifications and call of deacons is 1 Timothy 3:8-13.

> *Deacons likewise must be dignified, not double-tongued, not addicted to much wine, not greedy for dishonest gain. ⁹They must hold the mystery of the faith with a clear conscience. ¹⁰And let them also be tested first; then let them serve as deacons if they prove themselves blameless. ¹¹Their wives likewise must be dignified, not slanderers, but sober-minded, faithful in all things. ¹²Let deacons each be the husband of one wife, managing their children and their own households well. ¹³For those who serve well as deacons gain a good standing for themselves and also great confidence in the faith that is in Christ Jesus.*

10.2 Characteristics of a Deacon

The qualifications for a deacon parallel those for an elder in almost every way. However, he does not need to have the ability to teach, nor is the qualification to deal gently and hospitably with others mentioned. This likely reflects that the deacon is not expected to have the same intensity of interaction with people required of an elder.[6] However, this office is not merely one that deals with the physical needs of the church; most of these requirements relate to character and maturity, important characteristics for a man given a spiritual charge.[7] Deacons must hold to the gospel with integrity, they must be proven, and they must be examples in home life. While all believers are called as "deacons" in the general sense, official deacons must set a pace for maturity in Christ.

10.2.1 "Dignified" (1 Tim. 3:8)

"Dignified" connotes a sobriety of purpose and earnestness of conduct worthy of respect and winsome to others that brings honor to Christ and the office of deacon.

10.2.2 "Not double-tongued" (1 Tim. 3:8)

---

[6] Knight 167.
[7] J. R. W. Stott, (1996). *Guard the Truth: The message of 1 Timothy & Titus*. The Bible Speaks Today (99). Downers Grove, IL: InterVarsity Press.

The deacon is to speak in a sincere and holy manner. He is not to engage in gossip, slander, or deceit.

10.2.3 "Not addicted to much wine" (1 Tim. 3:8)

The self-mastery of previous characteristics makes it clear that a deacon should not be mastered by wine, drugs, or any other substance, but Paul makes it explicit here. We might add other potentially "addictive" types of activities such as gambling, pornography, computer gaming, or any activity that has overflowed its boundaries in the man's life.

10.2.4 Not greedy for dishonest gain" (1 Tim. 3:8)

There are different ways to be disqualified because a man is a "lover of money." It can mean a general greed that motivates someone to exploit the church for his own financial gain (Titus 1:7; 1 Pet. 5:2), or worse, to steal from it (Eph. 4:28). It can also mean a "covetousness" in the man's life that is really a form of "idolatry" (Col. 3:5), or it could simply be a continual discontentment with what God has provided for him (Phil. 4:10-13; Heb. 13:5). All of these are temptations for everyone, but when they are characteristic of a man, he should not serve as a deacon.

10.2.5 "Must hold the mystery of the faith with a clear conscience" (1 Tim. 3:9)

Deacons are to hold to the Christian faith with fidelity of doctrine and life in such a way that they can operate with a clear conscience, not condemned for heresy or immoral conduct.

10.2.6 "Tested first...prove themselves blameless" (1 Tim. 3:10)

Deacons are to be tested before they are selected for service in the office of deacon. They must be tested for character, doctrine, and conduct in a probationary period. If they qualify according to the biblical standards in a blameless way, then they can serve.

10.2.7 "Husband of one wife" (1 Tim. 3:12)

The requirement here does not speak to whether a man has been divorced or remarried, but, if he is married, speaks to a general faithfulness and sexual purity in his current marriage. The point is to examine his character, and a man's marriage reveals his character.

10.2.8 "Managing their children and their own households well" (1 Tim. 3:12)

The key word used in Timothy is "manage," a term that means "to exercise a position of leadership, rule, direct, be at the head of."[8] A man who manages his household well is obedient to the commandments related to his role as a father and husband: He is a husband who loves his wife as Christ loved the church (Eph. 5:25-33), he is living with her in an understanding way (1 Pet. 3:7), and he is a father who is bringing his children up in the discipline and instruction of the Lord (Eph. 6:4). In other words, there is a pattern of loving discipleship and gracious leadership in his management of the home.

10.3 The Role of a Deacon

Scripture does not provide great detail on the function of deacons. Some hold that the office is devoted primarily to meeting the temporal needs of the church. Others hold that the office involves any service that frees up the pastors to govern the church and devote themselves to the ministry of the Word and prayer (Acts 6:2-4). Either view is acceptable in Sovereign Grace. The character requirements in 1 Timothy 3 indicate the spiritual maturity the role demands and underline its significance for the life of the church (cf. Phil. 1:1). Deacons are not required to be able to teach, nor are they given the responsibility of church governance; those roles fall to elders/pastors/overseers. However, deacons can greatly bolster and support the role of the elders and the health of the congregation. They can do this by assuming responsibility for the leadership and care of the congregation in many areas in order to free elders to better lead in the ministry of the Word and prayer. Additionally, their involvement can help provide additional communication pathways with the congregation vital to a healthy, thriving church. This role may serve similarly to that of a ruling elder in some polities, albeit minus an official governing responsibility.

Although we wholeheartedly affirm the vital importance of the ministry of women in our churches, individual churches may differ on the acceptability of having women serve in the role of deacon. If a church decides to appoint women deacons, it is essential that the responsibilities of that role not violate other Scriptural commands that define and delineate the respective roles of men and women in the home and the church, particularly those that prohibit a woman from teaching or having authority over a man in the home or church (1 Tim. 2:12; cf. 1 Cor. 11:3).

---

[8] William Bauer, *A Greek-English Lexicon of the New Testament and Other Early Christian Literature,* 3rd. edition revised and edited by Frederick William Danker, based on previous work by W.F. Arndt, F.W. Gingrich, F.W. Danker (Chicago, IL: The University of Chicago Press, 2000), *proistēmi.*

11 The Role of the Congregation

11.1 Introduction

The following outline of the role of the congregation is not a comprehensive and exhaustive description of this essential aspect of church life. This *Book of Church Order* is oriented more toward the particulars of the exercise of church authority and not the other essential aspects of the life of a congregation. Accordingly and due to a desire to be economical this discussion is restricted to a limited number of short sections that directly impinge upon polity. Nevertheless, this material is given to provide a proper context to the exercise of church authority so that key roles of a congregation might be established.

It is important to distinguish between the vital roles and responsibilities of the entire congregation in the life and decision-making of the church versus granting an authority to the entire congregation to govern the local church. It is a noble biblical desire to ensure that all members of a church are properly exercising their gifts and contributing their voice to the life and decision-making of a church (cf. Acts 6:3, Acts 15:22, 1 Cor. 12:12-13:13, Matt. 18:15-20, 1 Tim. 5:19). Sadly, it is possible for pastors to domineer those in their charge (cf. 1 Peter 5:3, 2 John 9b, Acts 20:29). Therefore, it is imperative that pastors avoid leading in a domineering way or creating a church culture that does not foster vibrant congregational participation in the life of the church and in key decision-making for the whole church. However, accomplishing the goal of full biblical participation of the entire congregation does not mean that final governing authority must be handed over to the entire congregation.

Participation and final governing authority are separate issues and must not be confused if we are to understand and apply the biblical delineation of particular roles and offices in a local church (cf. Eph. 4:11-12, 1 Pet. 5:2, Phil. 1:1, 1 Tim. 5:17). While a healthy church will enjoy robust communication, cooperation, interdependence, and respect among all its members, including elders, deacons, and other congregants, this is not the same as experiencing an equal authority or responsibility to govern among all its members. Ultimately, elders must exercise their God-given authority in leading their local churches, albeit a biblically circumscribed, self-sacrificing, and humble authority (cf. 1 Pet. 5:1-3, John 10:11b, 2 Tim 2:24, 25). A congregation must correspondingly submit to its elders (cf. 1 Thess. 5:12-13; Heb 13:17). Such leadership and submission must be in the context of a vibrant, healthy, respectful, and fruitful participation for all members of the church. This section seeks to fill out a biblical understanding and practice for congregational participation within a conviction that elders are granted authority from God to govern the local church and must uniquely give account to God for their local church (cf. 1 Pet. 5:1-4; Heb. 13:17; Acts 20:28; 1 Cor. 3:10-17; etc.).

11.2 Congregational Equality

Church members do not have an inferior status to elders but are equal in standing before Christ and fellow members of his body. All members of the church—elders and congregants—are sheep under the authority of the Chief Shepherd and posses the same privileges: adoption by God, redemption by Christ, and sealing by the same Holy Spirit.

Therefore, there is no fundamental distinction among believers in Christ's body. All Christians—elders and congregants alike—have equal access to God through Christ (Gal. 3:28), are "priests" of God (1 Pet. 2:9), possess the Holy Spirit and spiritual gifts (Acts 2:17-18; 1 Cor. 6:19; 2 Cor. 1:22), receive illumination from the Spirit (1 Cor. 2:6-16), and enjoy all other spiritual blessings in Christ (Eph. 1:3ff.). All believers—elders and congregants alike—have access to God's Word and stand under its authority. As a result, the historical distinction between "clergy" and "laity" is an unbiblical idea that creates an illegitimate dichotomy within the body of Christ.

Each member plays an important role in the mission of the church. All Christians are indwelt by the Spirit of God, all are children of God, and all belong to the royal priesthood. Believers are called to a shared life together, involving fellowship, discipline, and care. While the church as a whole does not have responsibility for the governance of the church, each member contributes greatly to the health or demise of the church. The rule of elders in no way contradicts the prerogatives and liberties given to all who are in Christ.

11.3 Congregational Solidarity

Because elders are fundamentally a *part* of the congregation themselves, the relationship between elders and the congregation is meant to be one of joyful unity. Although elders must meet certain character qualifications, those qualifications are traits commanded of all believers. Elders have a responsibility to teach, but they, like the congregation, stand under the authority of God's Word. Elders are to proclaim and guard the gospel, but all believers are to stand firm in one spirit and strive together for the faith of the gospel (Phil. 1:27).

Pastoral instruction and leadership should seek to win a congregation's glad affirmation and forge a congregational solidarity through its manner of leadership. Such pastoral leadership includes:

- Humble instruction;
- Informative communication;
- Alerting the church to evidences of grace;
- Educating the church as to the fruit of its life, serving, and giving;
- Involving the church appropriately in the leadership's thinking and plans;
- Proactive deployment of people according to their gifts (Eph. 4:11ff.).

11.4 Congregational Responsibility

Because of the fundamental equality of believers, each member plays an important role in the mission of the church. Church members are called to a shared life together, involving fellowship, discipline, and care. Although the entire church does not have responsibility for the governance of the church, each member contributes greatly to the health or demise of the church. The rule of elders in no way contradicts the prerogatives and liberties given to all who are in Christ. Church members participate, under the leadership of the elders, in the joyful welcoming of new members and the excommunication of unfaithful members. The congregation is involved in the evaluation and affirmation of eldership candidates and has a responsibility to bring charges against a leader in serious sin. All believers are responsible to reject false teachers and unbiblical leadership. All believers have the right to approach God freely through Christ and to study the Scriptures for themselves. All believers are gifted by the Holy Spirit for active ministry in the church. Of course, the congregation must also recognize the value and role of elders in the church. We should pray for our leaders, maintain the unity of the Spirit with them, and joyfully submit to their biblical leadership.

At various points in the New Testament, the authors not only address the leaders of the churches to whom they write but the entire church as well. Consider Paul's letter to the Galatians. Paul is writing not only to the Galatian elders but to the whole church. He calls the church to be responsible to evaluate the teaching that comes from the pulpit. They are not to passively accept anything that comes out of the preacher's mouth but are to hold it up to the light of Christ and test it by his Word. If the teaching fails the test, the whole church is responsible to quit listening to the teacher—even if that teacher is an apostle like Paul himself.

> *I am astonished that you are so quickly deserting him who called you in the grace of Christ and are turning to a different gospel— [7]not that there is another one, but there are some who trouble you and want to distort the gospel of Christ. [8]But even if we or an angel from heaven should preach to you a gospel contrary to the one we preached to you, let him be accursed. [9]As we have said before, so now I say again: If anyone is preaching to you a gospel contrary to the one you received, let him be accursed. (Gal. 1:6-9)*

In 2 Timothy, Paul lays the responsibility for the presence of false teachers clearly at the foot of the congregation. They are the ones responsible for accumulating to themselves teachers in accordance with their own desires (4:3). They are the ones who do not endure sound doctrine, who want their ears tickled, and who consequently turn from truth to myths. They are the ones ultimately responsible for allowing their own desires to determine the kind of teachers they seek out for themselves.

> *Preach the word; be ready in season and out of season; reprove, rebuke, and exhort, with complete patience and teaching. [3]For the time*

is coming when people will not endure sound teaching, but having itching ears they will accumulate for themselves teachers to suit their own passions. (2 Tim. 4:2-3)

Although authority in the local church is given to elders, they are not to be insulated from the congregation's appropriate observations and concerns and even responsibility to ensure the fidelity of their leaders. Because Scripture affirms the right of church members to bring legitimate allegations concerning an elder (1 Tim. 5:19-21), a church's local polity in conjunction with the Sovereign Grace Rules of Discipline (which follow) outline the relevant policies and procedures by which such allegations can be evaluated. Clear communication about such avenues of recourse will foster both a healthy accountability and an atmosphere of trust. Additionally, the roles and responsibilities of the congregation may be worked out in Sovereign Grace churches by the following pursuits:

- Seeking input from the congregation for any pastoral candidate for ordination.
- Seeking input from the congregation for any deacon candidate for installation.
- Creating a church environment where there are vital relationships, active discussion, and cooperation between the elders and the whole church with a clear, comprehensive, and welcoming feedback system.
- Providing regular forums of communication and interaction as appropriate.
- Establishing and training the church in the use of the channels for feedback and redress outlined by local church policy and the policy and procedures of the Sovereign Grace *Book of Church Order*.
- Utilizing a formal and public affirmation process for key church decisions such as installing elders and deacons, approving an annual budget, making major changes in church by-laws, implementing major changes in church ministries, enforcing church discipline, and accepting church members. Such affirmation is permissible as long it is not technically binding (see BCO-12), does not nullify the authority of the elders to govern the church nor contradict this *Book of Church Order*.

A dynamic relationship of mutual care and respect and the leadership of godly elders is necessary for a healthy church polity. No church polity will work without the necessary qualifying character on the part of the pastors and the correspondent faith-filled submission of the congregation.

11.5 Congregational Submission

Within the general equality of all believers, God orders and gives leaders to his church. The congregation's submission to Christ finds expression in its submission to godly elders (1 Thess. 5:12-13; Heb. 13:17; 1 Pet. 5:5). All ministry to the church is ultimately *Christ's own ministry* and, as gifts from God, elders are an extension of Christ's ministry to his people.

Jesus is the apostle (Heb. 3:1), the prophet (Matt. 13:57), the teacher (Matt. 10:24-25), the shepherd (John 10:11; 1 Pet. 5:4), the evangelist (Luke 4:18), the preacher

(Matt. 4:17), and the servant (Mark 10:45). All leaders in the church carry on Jesus' own ministry.

This is a voluntary submission which must not be coerced and which assumes that elders are serving as faithful examples and are faithfully leading the congregation in obedience to God's Word. God's Word circumscribes the elders' authority. Only Scripture can bind the conscience of the Christian, and we forfeit our authority when we deviate from God's Word.

Biblical texts that specifically address the notion of authority with respect to the congregation and its leaders affirm elder rule and congregational submission:

- Elders rule/govern/manage (*proïstēmi*): 1 Tim. 3:4-5; 5:17; 1 Thess. 5:12; Rom. 12:8
- Elders lead (*hēgeomai*): Heb. 13:7, 17, 24
- Elders exercise oversight (*episkopos*; *episkopeō*): Acts 20:28; Phil. 1:1; Titus 1:7; 1 Pet. 5:2
- The congregation respects (lit. "know": *oida*[9]): 1 Thess. 5:12
- The congregation esteems (lit. "think, consider": *hēgeisthai*[10]): 1 Thess. 5:13
- The congregation obeys (*peithō*): Heb. 13:17
- The congregation submits (*hypeikō*): Heb. 13:17
- The congregation imitates (*mimeomai*): Heb. 13:7; 1 Cor. 11:1; 2 Thess. 3:7, 9

---

[9] The verb "to know" has the sense here of "take note of with a view to respecting and appreciating" (G.K. Beale, *1-2 Thessalonians* (IVP New Testament Commentary; Downers Grove, IL: InterVarsity, 2003), 160).

[10] "The combination of this verb "consider" with the adverb "quite beyond all measure" (*hyperekperissou*) yields the sense reflected in the NIV. The Thessalonians should think about them in the highest way possible, and so *hold them in highest regard*" (Gene L. Green, *The Letters to the Thessalonians* (Pillar New Testament Commentary; Grand Rapids: Eerdmans, 2002), 250-251).

12 Local Church Practices

12.1 Local Church Bylaws

In keeping with these principles, although a church may have formal congregational feedback, no congregational vote shall be regarded as binding in any Sovereign Grace church. While full and vibrant congregational participation is necessary for healthy church life, it does not necessitate congregational governance of the local church. Introducing binding congregational voting would introduce a conflicting practice of church governance that would eventually have to be resolved by resting final church authority either with the congregation or with its elders. Although we respect the many churches that practice church governance that puts the final authority in the hands of congregants, we believe it will be more consistent, more fruitful, and less problematic within our polity overall to rest final authority with the elders. We believe practicing elder rule in conjunction with vibrant congregational participation is the best application of biblical polity. Therefore, to be consistent with this conviction and practice, we have deemed that local church bylaws of Sovereign Grace churches must address the following key items.

12.1.1 Consistency with Book of Church Order

The constitution and bylaws of each local church must be fully consistent with the general principles and prescriptions of the *Sovereign Grace Book of Church Order*. Each church will have one year from the date of signing (or ratifying) the Sovereign Grace Partnership Agreement to bring their church bylaws into conformity with the *Book of Church Order*. It is highly recommended that each church take the initiative to have their bylaws reviewed by their Regional Judicial Review Committee in order to identify any areas that might need adjustment prior to signing the partnership agreement.

12.1.2 Local Elders have Sole Authority Over

The eldership of each local church has sole authority to write or change the local church's constitution and bylaws.

12.1.3 Regional Judicial Review Committee May Examine

The Regional Judicial Review Committee may examine the consistency of a local church's bylaws with *The Book of Church Order* if the Committee deems it necessary. If the Committee finds that a local church's bylaws are inconsistent with *The Book of Church Order*, and if after thorough discussion the local eldership refuses to change the bylaws accordingly, then this refusal may become grounds for pursuing a course of action as described in BCO-25.2.11-12.

PART TWO – Local Church Polity Section 12 – Local Church Practices

12.2 Official Membership

12.2.1 In accordance with the teaching of Scripture, converts to the church universal are added to a particular local church (Acts 2:41). It is within the context of that local church that they submit to specific local elders, who watch over their souls and must give an account (Hebrews 13:17, 1 Peter 5:3).

12.2.2 The identification of a believer with a specific local church and eldership requires a defined local membership. As a result, each Sovereign Grace church will actively maintain an official membership to which new members are added when they willingly join.

12.3 Solemnization of Marriage

12.3.1 Marriage is an institution designed and ordained by God though not a sacrament of the church.

12.3.2 The biblical definition of marriage is the exclusive sexual, procreative, and lifelong covenantal union of one person born biologically male and one person born biologically female.[11]

12.3.3 Sovereign Grace Churches prohibits its elders from officiating and affirming any marriage outside of the biblical definition of marriage set forth in BCO-12.3.2—including but not limited to same sex-marriages or unions, polygamous marriages, transgender marriages,[12] or marriages where one or both individuals have undergone a gender change. Sovereign Grace Churches believes there is a God-ordained link between one's biological sex and one's self-conception as male or female.

12.4 Reporting the Sexual Abuse of a Child (or a minor under 18 years of age).

Sovereign Grace churches and their elders have a moral obligation to protect children.

While reporting requirements related to child abuse vary from state to state, a Sovereign Grace elder who, in the course of his ministry involvement in a Sovereign Grace church, has cause to believe that a child is the victim of sexual abuse, then he must report such abuse to the appropriate child protection or law enforcement authorities.

This obligation exists whether the incidence occurs outside or inside the church or ministry. (Example of an 'outside' incident: a child or teen reports that he or

---

[11] This statement speaks to the basic understanding of what is meant by "marriage," though we acknowledge that in a given marriage not all of these elements will be necessarily fulfilled.

[12] A "transgender marriage" in this sentence means one where one or both parties is identifying as a gender different from his or her biological/birth sex. The next phrase ("or marriages where one or both…gender change") covers circumstances in which there has been an attempted "gender change" surgery to a gender other than one's biological/birth sex.

she has been sexually abused by a family member or friend. Example of an 'inside' incident: a child or teen reports that he or she has been sexually abused by a church staff member or volunteer.)

In addition, if a Sovereign Grace elder has cause to believe from an adult who was a victim of sexual abuse as a child that another child is currently at risk for sexual abuse by the same perpetrator, then the elder must notify the appropriate child protection or law enforcement authorities.

Each Sovereign Grace church must train church staff members and children's ministry workers to promote sexual abuse awareness and the safety of children involved in ministry programs and is solely responsible for the content and participation in such training.

By this we hope to protect children and promote justice in all our churches.

PART THREE: Extra-Local Polity

13 Regional Assemblies of Elders

13.1 Defining a Region

13.1.1 A Region is comprised of 5–20 Sovereign Grace churches within a designated geographical area. Temporary exceptions to these size limits may be made with the permission of the Leadership Team and the majority vote of the respective Regional Assembly of Elders. Sovereign Grace churches are only those churches whose elders have signed the appropriate Partnership Agreement and who have been accepted and approved by their Regional Assembly of Elders.

13.1.2 The Regional Assembly of Elders consists of all the elders of the local churches in a given Region (although at most five elders from each church shall be voting members). It is the primary place of support, care, accountability, and cooperation in mission outside of the local church. The responsibility for the mutual care and support of churches within a Region is not merely given a single man but rather falls to the entire Regional Assembly of Elders as a body.

13.1.3 Regions will be organized primarily on the basis of geographical considerations but may also include linguistic considerations.

13.1.4 New and Provisional Regions

13.1.4.1 New regions may be formed around the world. This will be facilitated by the Leadership Team.

13.1.4.2 Provisional regions may be formed around the world. A provisional region is one that is operating with certain authorized exceptions to *Book of Church Order* according to BCO-19.1. This will be facilitated by the Leadership Team subject to the approval of a simple majority of the Council of Elders.

13.1.5 Any realignment of a Region or additions to Regions must be approved by a majority vote of the pastors within the current Region.

13.1.5.1 An existing church or a church in an area where a plant or adoption is being proposed or is in process may switch regions by a simple majority vote of both Regional Assembly of Elders involved. The appropriate Leadership Team member will work with the respective Regional Leaders prior to any vote to facilitate such transfers.

13.1.5.2 Transfers of areas and/or churches from one region to another will be restricted to areas which border the region receiving that area.

13.1.6 Regional Assemblies shall meet at least once per year. When possible, this meeting shall occur with a majority of regional elders present in person.

13.1.7 A quorum consists of at least half of the voting members of the Regional Assembly of Elders. A quorum must be present for all binding votes. Being "present" means individual members participate either <u>in person</u> or via telephone/teleconference.

13.1.8 Regional Assemblies must conduct their business in person or teleconference when it concerns their essential functions: BCO-13.2.1-13.2.8. Yet, for certain trivial business items they may conduct matters through email. Such trivial items include approval of minutes, setting meeting dates and times, and approving a budget. It is also allowable to conduct matters by email if the Regional Assembly decides to do so by unanimous consent.

13.2 Responsibilities of the Regional Assemblies of Elders

Although all manner of informal fellowship, cooperation, and mutual care among the churches and elders of a Regional Assembly are encouraged, the official prerogatives of the Regional Assemblies of Elders are strictly limited to the following areas:

13.2.1 Approval of all candidates for eldership

13.2.1.1 Only the eldership of a local church can ordain new elders (BCO-1.3). Therefore, the local eldership bears primary responsibility for examining the life and doctrine of candidates for pastoral ministry in order to determine whether the candidate meets the biblical character qualifications (BCO-3) and fully agrees with the Sovereign Grace *Statement of Faith*. However, the elder candidate must be examined and approved by the Regional Assembly of Elders and its Ordination Committee before he may be ordained in the local church (BCO-1.1; BCO-9.3.6).

13.2.1.2 Ordination examinations will be standardized within all Sovereign Grace Regions. The Leadership Team of Sovereign Grace will be charged with compiling ordination exams for use by the Regional Assemblies of Elders after such exams have been approved by the Council of Elders and Regional Assemblies of Elders (BCO-15.3.8).

13.2.1.3 The Region's Ordination Committee (see BCO-13.2.7.1.a) shall administer the written and oral exams to the candidate (BCO-9.3.6).

13.2.1.4 Once the candidate passes the written and oral exams he must affirm in writing that he fully subscribes to the *Statement of Faith* and that he will submit without exception to the

Sovereign Grace Book of Church Order. If he has exceptions to either he must declare those in writing to the Regional Assembly of Elders (BCO-9.3.6). Once these steps are completed the Ordination Committee shall present the candidate to the Regional Assembly of Elders with its recommendation.

The Regional Elders may question the candidate concerning his doctrine or life as the Assembly deems necessary. After questioning, the Regional Assembly will vote (according to 13.1.8) on whether the candidate may be ordained. A simple majority is required for approval (BCO-9.3.6).

13.2.1.5 The Regional Elders or Ordination Committee must demonstrate just cause to reject a candidate who has been previously vetted by his local church and has passed the required ordination examinations. Just cause must consist exclusively of either heterodoxy (i.e., deviation from the *Sovereign Grace Statement of Faith*) or scandalous or serious sin (BCO-9.3.6)

13.2.1.6 As per BCO-9.7, when a Sovereign Grace elder from outside the Region is called to serve at a local church within the Region, the Regional Assembly of Elders must review the elder's exceptions to the *Statement of Faith* or the explicitly mandated practices of *The Book of Church Order* and determine their significance.

13.2.1.7 See BCO-2 through BCO-10 on Local Elders and especially BCO-9.3.6 on ordination.

13.2.2 Adjudications within the Region

13.2.2.1 Each Regional Assembly of Elders will appoint a qualified sitting Judicial Review Committee that is trained in ecclesiastical law and procedure by the Sovereign Grace Court of Appeals or their delegates. This training must be completed within 18 months of being appointed to the Regional Judicial Review Committee.

13.2.2.2 Each Regional Judicial Review Committee will consist of five to seven elders, preferably from different churches, only three of whom will serve on any single case. This is to provide for enough Judicial Review Committee members to avoid conflicts of interest and allow for necessary recusals.

13.2.2.3 The Judicial Review Committee will supply a Moderator who will review the plaintiff's charge and evidence when a charge is brought against an elder (as described in BCO-24.3-4). The Moderator may dismiss the charge if he deems that it does not warrant a trial.

13.2.2.4 This Judicial Review Committee will hear cases relating to the discipline of a congregant (BCO-23; BCO-25.2.3) or elder (BCO-24.4; BCO-24.6.6; BCO-24.7.3; BCO-24.12; BCO-25.2.4-5) that are appealed from a local church within the Region.

13.2.2.5 If necessary, the members of this Judicial Review Committee will supply members for a local Panel to try charges brought against elders. If no local elders are available to serve on a Panel, the Judicial Review Committee will assume jurisdiction (cf. BCO-22.1.2-3).

13.2.2.6 This Judicial Review Committee will be a place of appeal for any elder who is removed by a local Panel (cf. BCO-24.6.6; BCO-24.12; BCO-25.2.5).

13.2.2.7 This Judicial Review Committee may also hear and adjudicate, if it deems them credible, any complaints or grievances against a local eldership by a member of a local church within the Region (BCO-25.2.10.2-3).

13.2.2.8 From among the members of the Judicial Review Committees, the Sovereign Grace Nominating Committee will nominate and Sovereign Grace Council of Elders will confirm the members of the Sovereign Grace Court of Appeal (for the confirmation process, see BCO-15.3.1.2; the Court of Appeal is explained in BCO-26). The intention of these selections is to provide the best adjudicators to serve on the Court of Appeal.

13.2.2.9 See BCO-25, "Regional Judicial Review Committees."

13.2.3 Discipline of an Eldership within the Region

13.2.3.1 A censure is an official reprimand of erring parties, a statement of rebuke or disapproval. It is intended to clarify relevant concerns, to produce repentance, and to protect the broader church. Censures are one expression of the doctrinal and moral accountability that the local churches of the New Testament enjoyed among themselves. Censure provides a method of warning and restoring the wayward, short of removal. This promotes the glory of God and the health of Sovereign Grace churches. Censure is not intended to tear down the church, but rather to build up and restore the church. Reprimands of this nature should be given in a spirit of Christian love, with impartiality, sobriety, and a concern for the glory of Christ in the church.

13.2.3.2 A Sovereign Grace church's eldership may be censured by the Regional Assembly of Elders if it is determined that the elders of that church have persistently strayed from the *Sovereign Grace Statement of Faith* or *Book of Church Order* or have conducted themselves in an egregiously sinful manner (see BCO-20; BCO-25.2.10.4-6).

13.2.3.3 If an eldership does not respond to censure, the Regional Assembly of Elders may revoke its approval of the ordination of those elders. Sovereign Grace thereby ceases to recognize those men as elders. The Regional Assembly of Elders will assume pastoral responsibility for the church's members (as described in BCO-9). On the disavowal of an eldership, see BCO-25.2.11.

13.2.3.4 Every Sovereign Grace church eldership will have the right of biblical due process in the case of censure or removal (BCO-25.2.11.5).

13.2.4 Church Planting

The Regional Assembly of Elders administrates Sovereign Grace church planting within the Region in order to wisely dispense shared financial resources and maintain a unified, cohesive strategy for advancing the mission within a given geographical area. The Sovereign Grace Director of Church Planting and Missions will assist Regions in church planting, bringing expertise, experience, and initiative to this task.

13.2.4.1 Working in conjunction with the Sovereign Grace Director of Church Planting & Missions, the Regional Assembly of Elders will have the responsibility to identify and approve, by a simple majority vote, all locations for Sovereign Grace church plants within the Region.

13.2.4.2 Churches beginning exploratory Sovereign Grace church planting initiatives such as campuses, mission churches, or other Sovereign Grace works, will communicate the plans and intentions of such works to the Regional Leader and the Regional Church Planting Committee prior to their start.

13.2.4.2.a The Regional Leader and Regional Church Planting Committee will work together with the initiating church to develop an appropriate approach for informing the region of the work. This may include steps up to and including a formal report at the Regional Assembly of Elders and opportunity for the Regional Assembly of Elders to comment on and affirm the exploratory work as part of the larger regional mission strategy.

13.2.4.2.b The Regional Church Planting Committee is responsible for guiding an exploratory work to best position it for its eventual approval as a new church in the region. The Regional Church Planting Committee will guide the process in accordance with church planting and adoption provisions of the *Book of Church Order* so that the Regional Assembly of Elders may have confidence that all new churches and pastors have been appropriately evaluated and vetted for approval by the region.

13.2.4.3 Although the Regional Assembly of Elders must approve every Sovereign Grace church plant (i.e., one utilizing Sovereign Grace funds and intending to become a member of Sovereign Grace Churches from its inception) by a simple majority vote, it may delegate exploratory work to its Regional Church Planting Committee (see BCO-13.2.7.1.c) or to the Sovereign Grace Director of Church Planting & Missions.

13.2.4.4 If a church desires to plant a church that will not be part of Sovereign Grace and will not utilize Sovereign Grace funds, it is free to do so without the involvement or approval of the Regional Assembly of Elders.

13.2.4.5 A church plant becomes an official Sovereign Grace church with all its privileges and responsibilities when its elder/eldership signs the appropriate Partnership Agreement (see BCO-19), and it has been accepted and approved by its Regional Assembly of Elders.

13.2.5 Church Adoptions

13.2.5.1 Overview: The Regional Church Planting Committee, the Regional Ordination Committee, and the Regional Judicial Review Committee, have the joint responsibility to ensure that a church and eldership being recommended for adoption in a region conforms to the guidelines of *The Book of Church Order*. The Regional Leader will take responsibility to coordinate the work of the committees and in communication between the candidate church and the region and its committees.

13.2.5.2 Role of the Leadership Team and the Director of Church Planting and Mission: As an extension of the Leadership Team, the Director of Church Planting and Mission will assist the work of the Regional Leader and Regional committees. The Director of Church Planting and Mission will maintain a Guidelines & Best Practices document to serve Sovereign Grace in the adoption process. This document will provide the basis for an assessment and recommended path for all adoptions. An initial self-assessment and interview with the church adoption candidate by the Director of Church Planting and Mission or his delegate will take place to provide preliminary information. A report will be sent to the Regional

Leader, Regional Church Planting Committee, and the Regional Ordination Committee indicating strengths, weaknesses, and potential concerns. The authority to approve or reject the church adoption rests solely with the Regional Assembly of Elders.

13.2.5.3 Role of the Regional Church Planting Committee: The Regional Church Planting Committee, facilitated by the Regional Leader, will conduct a full assessment of the church's compatibility with our theology, mission, values, and polity based on the process laid out in the Guidelines and Best Practices for Adoptions document. They will submit their assessment and recommendations to the Regional Leader.

13.2.5.4 Role of the Regional Ordination Committee: The Regional Ordination Committee, facilitated by the Regional Leader, will assess the doctrine of the candidate church elders. The elder(s) of the candidate church must be reviewed for transfer and confirmation of ordination by the Ordination Committee. The Ordination Committee will make a recommendation to the Regional Assembly of Elders for or against the transfer of each elder's ordination status. The Regional Ordination Committee may recommend to the Regional Assembly of Elders that the elder(s) of the candidate church pass the Sovereign Grace Ordination Standards and Exams if it judges this prudent. The candidate church elder(s) must each sign the following statements:

> *"I declare sincerely before God that I believe that all the articles and points of doctrine contained in the Sovereign Grace Statement of Faith fully agree with the Scriptures, and I own that Statement as the statement and confession of my faith. These are doctrines I promise to teach and defend in public and in private. I promise further that if in the future I come to have reservations about any of these doctrines, I will share these reservations with my eldership and the Regional Assembly of Elders.*
>
> *If ordained, I will submit to the explicitly mandated polity practices of the Sovereign Grace Book of Church Order. I affirm that the form of government contained in the Sovereign Grace Book of Church Order is a wise and suitable application of Scriptural principle."*

If the candidate has any reservations about or takes any exceptions to either the *Statement of Faith* or the explicitly mandated practices of *The Book of Church Order*, he must inform his local eldership and the Regional Assembly of Elders.

These exceptions must be submitted in writing, and each elder's exceptions shall be kept on record with the local eldership, the Regional Assembly of Elders, and Sovereign Grace.

The local eldership shall first investigate the exception before presenting the candidate to the Regional Assembly of Elders. The Regional Assembly of Elders shall determine the significance of the candidate's exceptions. If the exception is a trivial or semantic and not a substantive difference with any doctrine in the *Statement of Faith* or explicitly mandated practice in *The Book of Church Order*, then the candidate may sign the above statements and be put forward for a vote on his ordination. However, if it is determined that the candidate substantially disagrees with any of the doctrines of the *Statement of Faith* or the explicitly mandated practices in *The Book of Church Order*, he may not be approved for ordination. The Ordination Committee shall recommend to him a course of study on the relevant doctrines and principles, if the candidate is willing, in the hopes that his exceptions might be overcome.

The report of the Committee, which will include the recommendations of the Regional Ordination Committee, the signed statements from the candidate elder(s), and any exceptions discovered in this process, will be delivered to the Regional Leader and the Regional Church Planting Committee.

13.2.5.5 Role of the Regional Judicial Review Committee: The Regional Judicial Review Committee, facilitated by the Regional Leader, will assess whether the candidate church's governing documents are in compliance with *The Book of Church Order*. They will submit their assessment and recommendations to the Regional Leader and the Regional Church Planting Committee.

13.2.5.6 Reports to the Regional Assembly of Elders: The Regional Leader will gather the assessment reports of the Regional Church Planting Committee, the Regional Ordination Committee, and the Regional Judicial Review Committee and then submit these to the Regional Assembly of Elders. These must be submitted at least 30 days prior to a vote on the ordination(s) and adoption of the candidate church.

13.2.5.7 Role of Regional Assembly of Elders: Before there can be a final vote on the ordination of any candidate elder(s) the Regional Assembly may have to rule on issues raised by the Committee Reports. They must also rule on any exceptions that the candidate elders took to the *Statement of Faith* and the *Book of Church Order* (cf. BCO-9.3.6). If all such matters are resolved, then they move to vote on the ordination transfer of the candidate elders. Adequate discussion is required before any vote. Transferring the ordination of these elders requires a simple majority. The Regional Assembly then votes on whether to adopt the church, which requires a two-thirds majority.

13.2.5.8 The adoption is finalized when the Partnership Agreement is signed by all necessary parties (Executive Director, Regional Leader, Elders of the Partner Church).

13.2.5.9 If a church without elders seeks adoption in Sovereign Grace and the Region votes to adopt it, then the church will come under the pastoral care of the Regional Assembly until elders can be found (as described in BCO-9.5).

13.2.6 Care for Churches and Pastors within the Region

13.2.6.1 The Regional Assembly of Elders has a shared responsibility for the health and vitality of each church within the Region.

13.2.6.2 This care may be expressed in a variety of ways including counsel and advice, sending representatives to speak and minister at the request of the local church elders, and through cooperative conferences and Regional Assembly of Elders meetings.

13.2.6.3 Regional Leaders will facilitate this care within each Region.

13.2.7 Selection of Regional Officers and Committees and Delegation of Their Authority

13.2.7.1 In order to organize for certain essential functions on the Regional level, every Regional Assembly of Elders will have the following committees:

13.2.7.1.a Ordination Committee (at least three members): Conducts all ordination reviews and examinations on behalf of the Regional Assembly of Elders. The term of office will be 3 years. There are no limitations on the number of terms that an elder may serve. If a committee member resigns his position or is removed from his position, then, after recommendations from the Regional Nominating Committee, the Regional Assembly will elect another elder to serve the remainder of the term as needed.

13.2.7.1.b Judicial Review Committee (five to seven members): Conducts all adjudications at the Regional level. The term of office will be 6 years. There are no limitations on the number of terms that an elder may serve. If a committee member resigns his position or is removed from his position, then, after recommendations from the Regional Nominating Committee, the Regional Assembly will elect another elder to serve the remainder of the term as needed.

13.2.7.1.c Church Planting Committee (at least three members): Works with the Director of Church Planting and Missions to identify and approve all new church plants within the Region. The term of office will be 3 years. There are no limitations on the number of terms that an elder may serve. If a committee member resigns his position or is removed from his position, then, after recommendations from the Regional Nominating Committee, the Regional Assembly will elect another elder to serve the remainder of the term as needed.

13.2.7.1.d Regional Nominating Committee (three members): Researches, identifies, and nominates the best candidates for the Regional Leader and the members of the Region's various committees. These committee members must be elected or confirmed by the Regional Assembly of Elders and should include the most experienced and most capable leaders within the Region. Any elder within the Region may nominate a man for this Committee. When the Nominating Committee nominates a candidate, he must still be approved by a simple majority of the Regional Assembly of Elders present and voting. The term of office will be 3 years. There are no limitations on the number of terms that an elder may serve. If a committee member resigns his position or is removed from his position, then, after recommendations from the Regional Nominating Committee, the Regional Assembly will elect another elder to serve the remainder of the term as needed.

13.2.7.1.e Regional Budget Committee (at least three members): Assists the Regional Leader in proposing and presenting a yearly budget to the Regional Assembly of Elders for discussion and a vote of affirmation. Affirmation requires a simple majority. This committee will follow best practices established in cooperation with the Leadership

Team. The term of service for this committee is three years. There are no limitations on the number of terms that an elder may serve. If a committee member resigns his position or is removed from his position, then, after recommendations from the Regional Nominating Committee, the Regional Assembly will elect another elder to serve the remainder of the term as needed.

13.2.7.2 In order to facilitate unofficial functions every Region may establish ad hoc committees or working groups:

13.2.7.2.a Members of an ad hoc committee do not need to be nominated by the Regional Nominating Committee.

13.2.7.2.b The purpose of an ad hoc committee should defined and its duration specified.

13.2.7.2.c Ad hoc committees established within a region serve in an advisory and assistant capacity, not in the stead of the Regional Assembly of Elders or its standing committees, nor can they be empowered with any authority already allocated in the *Book of Church Order*.

13.2.7.2.d These ad hoc committees are to serve short term purposes. Any committee designed to serve more than one year must be approved by the Regional Assembly of Elders and the members of such a committee must be elected by simple majority vote of Regional Assembly of Elders.

13.2.7.2.e The creation of ad hoc committees, its members, its purpose, and its duration shall be recorded in the Regional meeting official minutes.

13.2.7.3 Every Region will select one man to be the Regional Leader (cf. BCO-14).

13.2.7.3.a The Region's Nominating Committee, with the counsel and advice of the Sovereign Grace Leadership Team, will put forward a qualified candidate to be confirmed by a majority vote of the Regional Assembly of Elders.

13.2.7.3.b The Regional Leader will be selected by the Regional Assembly of Elders every four years.

13.2.7.3.c A Regional Leader will serve a four-year term and may serve multiple terms without limits.

13.2.7.3.d If a Regional Leader is unable to complete his term, the Regional Assembly of Elders will select his replacement.

13.2.8 Approval of Changes to the Sovereign Grace *Statement of Faith*

13.2.8.1 Three-fourths of the Regional Assemblies of Elders must approve by a simple majority vote any changes to the Sovereign Grace *Statement of Faith* (BCO-15.3.2-3).

13.2.8.2 This also requires a three-fourths majority vote of those present and voting at the Council of Elders (see BCO-15.3.2 for the entire process).

13.2.9 Minutes

Minutes must be taken at all official business meetings of the Regional Assemblies of Elders and of the Regional Committees. These need not be word-for-word transcripts, but they should include at least (1) the official agenda, (2) decisions made and votes taken, (3) a summary of the major points brought up in debate or discussion, and (4) any statement, especially of dissent or protest, that a member requests be included in the minutes. Minutes for Regional committee meetings will be approved by the members of the respective committee. Minutes for the Regional Assembly of Elders Meetings must be approved by the Regional Judicial Review Committee and be responsibly archived.

14 Regional Leaders

14.1 The Purpose of Regional Leaders

The Regional Leader is to use his leadership gifts to inspire and impart vision to the elders in his region, resulting in joyful participation in our shared mission and appreciation of our shared doctrine and values. He is to motivate, encourage and exhort the elders of his region to fulfill our shared commitments and warn them against cultural temptations or internal inconsistencies with our doctrine and values. He also represents the whole Regional Assembly of Elders in providing care, equipping, and counsel to the elders within the region.

Regional Leaders do not occupy a special "office" in addition to that of an elder but rather are elders whose gifting for broader leadership is recognized by the Regional Assembly of Elders. Therefore, the Regional Leader is recognized and elected by the elders in his region and is accountable to them. He also becomes their representative in the election of five members of the Sovereign Grace Nominating Committee from among the Regional Leaders. In essence, the Regional Leader (a) is a representative of his Regional Assembly of Elders to Sovereign Grace and (b) provides leadership and coordination of activities within his region.

14.2 Roles and Responsibilities of the Regional Leaders

14.2.1 Moderates Regional Assembly of Elders meetings;

14.2.2 Oversees the election or confirmation of committee members for the Region;

14.2.3 Represents the Regional Assembly of Elders at the installation of elders in the local church or, if unable to, appoints another elder within the Region to represent the Regional Assembly of Elders;

14.2.4 Coordinates the giving of aid, assistance, and advice to a church whose eldership is embroiled in controversy. Coordinates conciliation and mediation efforts for a church or eldership at the request of the eldership;

14.2.5 Facilitates the work of regional committees as needed. He can delegate this task as he sees fit;

14.2.6 Gives advice and encouragement to elders and elderships;

14.2.7 Coordinates care to churches and pastors within the Region. He may delegate some of his responsibilities to other pastors in the Region;

14.2.8 He represents his Regional Assembly of Elders when the Regional Leaders convene as necessary to elect their five members of the Sovereign Grace Nominating Committee (BCO-16.3.1);

14.2.9 His term is four years, with no limit on the number of terms he may serve;

14.2.10 He may be appropriately compensated for his work outside of his local church.

14.3 Qualifications of the Regional Leaders

14.3.1 He must have been a Sovereign Grace pastor for at least five years.

14.3.2 He must be relationally strong within the Region and able to facilitate strong gospel-centered unity.

14.3.3 He must be doctrinally strong and passionate about our shared values.

14.3.4 He must have experience in and a heart for Sovereign Grace.

14.3.5 He must be a recognized leader among leaders.

14.3.6 He must have a heart for and commitment to our mission to plant and care for churches.

14.3.7 He must have a teaching gift sufficient to bring strong, Scripturally-based leadership to the Region.

15 Council of Elders

Although the primary locus of integration, care, accountability, and support for the local church is the Regional Assembly of Elders, the Council of Elders provides another important point of support and fellowship and helps foster solidarity across Regions. As churches, we have historically shared a rich history of fellowship throughout the US and even globally. The Council of Elders is designed to foster our union with other Sovereign Grace churches in other Regions.

15.1 Formation

A designated representative from the eldership of each church will form the Council of Elders. Churches whose membership exceeds 500 adult (18 or more years old) members may send an additional representative elder.

15.1.1 Each Sovereign Grace church whose elders have signed the Partnership Agreement and has been accepted and approved by its Regional Assembly of Elders is a qualified member of the Sovereign Grace Churches and may send its representative elder(s) to the Council of Elders meeting.

15.1.2 To qualify as a representative to the Council of Elders, the representative elder must be an ordained Sovereign Grace elder in good standing with his Regional Assembly of Elders.

15.1.3 An elder who has been disavowed by either the Regional Judicial Review Committee or Sovereign Grace Court of Appeals may not serve as the representative to the Council of Elders neither may he participate in any Sovereign Grace Regional Assembly of Elders.

15.1.4 A church whose eldership has been disavowed and who does not follow the disavowed eldership may continue as a member of the Sovereign Grace Churches but will have no voting representative on the Council of Elders until a duly qualified elder is appointed.

15.1.5 A church may be removed as a member of the Sovereign Grace Churches if its members continue to follow the leadership of a disavowed eldership.

15.2 Annual and Special Meetings

15.2.1 The Executive Committee, on behalf of the Council of elders, will schedule and approve future Council of Elders meetings. The dates will be suggested by the Executive Director based on the most amenable date for the next Pastors Conference. The Executive Director will draft an agenda for the Council of Elders meeting, approved by the Leadership Team, and sent to all Council members 30 days prior to the scheduled Council of Elders Meeting.

15.2.2 Members of the Council of Elders may move to hold other meetings if they are necessary. If one fourth of the Council of Elders calls for a

Special Meeting of the Council of Elders, the Executive Committee must schedule the Special Meeting of the Council of Elders within 60 days of the request. Those elders initiating the request must present a unified agenda to the Executive Committee along with their petition for the meeting. The Executive Committee will send the proposed agenda and any supporting documentation to all Council members at least 30 days prior to the Special Meeting if the agenda does not involve any amendments to the *Book of Church Order*. If the agenda involves proposed amendments to the *Book of Church Order*, the elders initiating the request must submit the agenda along with the proposed amendments to the Executive Committee 45 days ahead of the meeting. The Executive Committee will then send them to the Council of Elders 30 days ahead of the meeting. Amendments to the *Statement of Faith* shall only be presented at the annual Council of Elders meeting.

15.2.3 A special meeting may not be called for the purpose of further debating a past decision by the Council of Elders or in order to impede an action already decided on by the Council of Elders. Once a decision has been made, it stands and must be acted on accordingly. A Special Meeting on a previous decision may only be called if conditions or circumstances have significantly changed. The Executive Committee has the authority to rule on whether a change is serious enough to warrant a Special Meeting. The Executive Committee may pursue counsel from whomever it deems advisable including the Polity Committee and Rules Committee.

15.2.4 The Executive Committee, by a majority vote of the Committee members, may call a Special Meeting of the Council of Elders if it deems it necessary. Notice of the Special Meeting will be sent to all Council members 30 days prior to the meeting with a detailed agenda of the Special Meeting and any supporting documents pertinent to the Council's business if the agenda does not involve any amendments to the *Book of Church Order*. If the agenda involves proposed amendments to the *Book of Church Order*, the Executive Committee will send them along with the agenda to the Council of Elders 30 days ahead of the meeting. Amendments to the *Statement of Faith* shall only be presented at the annual Council of Elders meeting.

15.2.5 A quorum consists of at least half of the members of the Council of Elders. A quorum must be present for all binding votes.

15.3 Responsibilities of the Council of Elders

The official prerogatives of the Council of Elders are strictly limited to the following:

15.3.1 The creation and confirmation of committees

15.3.1.1 The Council of Elders may create committees in order to expedite and facilitate the execution of its appointed tasks.

Any member of the Council of Elders may move to create a committee. The motion will stipulate the number of committee members, the length of their terms, and the committee's mandate. If the motion is seconded, the Council shall vote on the matter, which will be decided by a simple majority. The Council of Elders may decide to create ad-hoc committees that do not require the involvement of the Nominating Committee. This will be done according to *The Modern Rules of Order*.

15.3.1.2 The Nominating Committee of the Council of Elders (BCO-16.3) will nominate candidates to the committee. All committee candidates must be Sovereign Grace elders, although they need not be members of the Council. The candidates must each be confirmed by a simple majority vote of the Council of Elders.

    15.3.1.2.a Terms of service will begin January 1.

    15.3.1.2.b If a committee member is unable to complete his term, his committee will elect a replacement who will serve until the Council of Elders can meet to elect someone to a regular term.

    15.3.1.2.c Upon recommendation of the committee or three members of the council of Elders, committee members may be removed from office by a simple majority vote of the Council of Elders, effective immediately.

    15.3.1.2.d The Chairman of each Committee has authority to introduce business relevant to his Committee in meetings of the Council of Elders, even if he is not a member of the Council.

15.3.1.3 The Council of Elders will thus create a Polity Committee. It shall consist of 7 members whose terms will be 3 years each. There will be no limit on the number of terms that an elder may serve. If he is unable complete his term, then, upon the recommendation of the Sovereign Grace Nominating Committee, the Sovereign Grace Council of Elders will elect another to fulfill his office and term.

The Polity Committee's mandate will be to review the *Book of Church Order* and propose amendments as necessary and to fulfill whatever other polity needs that Sovereign Grace Churches may have, as deemed so by the Council of Elders.

The Polity Committee will also advise the Council on amendments to the *Book of Church Order* which may be proposed by other Council members (cf. BCO-15.3.4.7).

The Polity Committee shall also exercise oversight over the *Rules of Procedure for Adjudications* (cf. BCO-21.7). The Polity Committee may change the *Rules of Procedure* as it deems wise, and such changes are immediately binding without being subject to any further vote by the Council of Elders. Such changes must, however, be consistent with the *Book of Church Order*. The Council of Elders may nullify changes to the *Rules of Procedure* by simple majority vote. To nullify a change that the Polity Committee has made or to propose a new change to the *Rules of Procedure,* a member of the Council of Elders must submit their proposal to the entire Council of Elders 60 days in advance of the Council of Elders meeting.

15.3.1.4 The Council of Elders will also create a Theology Committee. This Committee will be chaired by the Director of Theology and Training and shall consist of 6 additional members whose terms will be 3 years each. There will be no limit on the number of terms that an elder may serve. The mandate of the Theology Committee will be to review the *Statement of Faith*, to propose amendments to it if necessary, to advise the Council on amendments to the *Statement of Faith* which may be proposed by other Council members (cf. BCO-15.3.2), to propose and amend Ordination Standards, and to fulfill whatever theological needs that Sovereign Grace Churches may have, as deemed so by the Council of Elders.

15.3.2 Proposal and approval of changes to the *Statement of Faith*

15.3.2.1 The Leadership Team, with leadership primarily coming from the Director of Theology, may initiate potential changes to the *Statement of Faith*.

15.3.2.2 Any three Council of Elders members may initiate potential changes to the *Statement of Faith.*

15.3.2.3 Potential changes must be submitted to the Executive Committee 90 days in advance of a Council of Elders meeting in order to give time for the proposed change to be studied. Dialogue between the Executive Committee and the party proposing the change may result in an edit or withdrawal of the proposal. If, however, the submitting elders do not edit or withdraw the request for the proposed change, the Executive Committee must put the proposed change on the agenda of the next Council meeting for consideration.

15.3.2.4 60 days in advance of the next Council of Elders meeting, every proposed change to the *Statement of Faith* must be sent to every member of the Council of Elders. At this meeting, the Council of Elders will vote on the merits of pursuing the proposed change. If one fourth of the Council of Elders votes in favor of pursuing it, the change will be sent to the Theology Committee for consideration.

15.3.2.5 The Theology Committee will study the change over the next year and will send its report and recommendation to the Council of Elders 90 days in advance of the Council's next meeting.

15.3.2.6 Council members may produce written responses to the Theology Committee's report for distribution to the Council 30 days prior to the Council's meeting.

15.3.2.7 For any change to be adopted, it must receive a three-fourths majority of the votes cast by the Council.

15.3.2.8 Any change that is approved by the Council of Elders must then be affirmed with a simple majority by three-fourths of all the Regional Assemblies of Elders. Every Regional Assembly must vote on the proposed change within a year of its approval by the Council of Elders. Each Regional Leader will immediately report the outcome of the vote to the Executive Director. The Executive Director will report the outcome of the votes in the Regional Assemblies at the next meeting of the Council of Elders. If the amendment has been approved, it shall at that time become a binding part of the *Statement of Faith*.

15.3.3 Process when two or more sections of the *Statement of Faith* are rewritten at once

15.3.3.1 A motion is introduced to rewrite two or more entire sections of the *Statement of Faith*. The process will then be guided by the Theology Committee. Changes of less than two entire sections are governed by BCO-15.3.2.

15.3.3.2 Each section must reach a level of contingent approval by the Council of Elders. Contingent approval requires:

15.3.3.2.a The Theology Committee first writes a draft of a new section.

15.3.3.2.b This new section is presented at a Council of Elders meeting and elderships then have 120 days to submit feedback on the drafted section.

15.3.3.2.c This feedback is considered by the Theology Committee and the drafted section is revised accordingly.

15.3.3.2.d This revised draft is then presented at a Council of Elders meeting.

15.3.3.2.e The Council will then open the floor for debate on the draft section, as organized by the Theology

Committee (paragraphs, sections, or all the revised sections at once). Debate will proceed as follows:

1. Council members will propose changes to the draft section and reasons for these changes.
2. The council will then debate and vote on whether these proposed changes are substantive enough to warrant opening the draft section to changes.
3. A majority vote is required to open a draft section to changes.
4. If the Council proceeds with such emendations, debate will be limited to one hour but can be extended by a majority vote of the Council of Elders.
5. Once all proposed changes have been debated and voted upon, a three-fourths majority is required to approve the newly revised (individual) section.

15.3.3.2.f   A three-fourths majority is required to approve the sections.

15.3.3.2.g   Sections that receive a three-fourths majority are then sent to the Regional Assemblies to be ratified within one year. At least three-fourths of the Regional Assemblies must approve the new sections by simple majority vote.

15.3.3.3   The Theology Committee may decide that sections given contingent approval earlier may need to be revised based on sections revised later in the process. If these are more than copy edits, a section must go through the process detailed above.

15.3.3.4   Once the sections have been approved by the Regional Assemblies, a majority vote by the Council of Elders will make these sections active as the current *Statement of Faith*.

15.3.3.5   The Theology Committee may make copy edits for grammar, punctuation, and spelling. The importance of the *Statement of Faith* even in its details means that these edits must be carefully considered. These will be sent to the elders and a meeting of the Council of Elders (annual or special) will approve them by unanimous consent. Such changes do not need to go through the full approval process detailed above (BCO-15.3.3.2).

15.3.4 Proposal and approval of changes to the *Sovereign Grace Book of Church Order*

    15.3.4.1 The Leadership Team, with leadership primarily coming from the Director of Theology, may initiate potential changes to the *Sovereign Grace Book of Church Order*.

    15.3.4.2 The Polity Committee may initiate changes to the *Sovereign Grace Book of Church Order*.

    15.3.4.3 Any three members of the Council of Elders may initiate potential changes to the *Sovereign Grace Book of Church Order*.

    15.3.4.4 The Executive Committee may initiate potential changes to the *Sovereign Grace Book of Church Order*.

    15.3.4.5 Potential changes must be submitted to the Executive Committee 90 days in advance of the annual Council of Elders meeting in order to give time for the proposed change to be studied and to get it on the Council's agenda.

    15.3.4.6 60 days in advance of the Council of Elders meeting, the proposed change must be sent to every member of the Council.

    15.3.4.7 The Polity Committee will be charged with the responsibility to study the proposed changes and give their reasoned input at the next Council meeting.

    15.3.4.8 For any change to be adopted, it must receive a simple majority of the votes cast by the Council of Elders.

    15.3.4.9 All approved changes to the *Sovereign Grace Book of Church Order* will be sent to every Sovereign Grace church elder.

    15.3.4.10 The Polity Committee is responsible to incorporate newly approved amendments into the *Book of Church Order*. They have the ability to **copy** edit these amendments to (1) adjust incorrect grammar and (2) make the style consistent with the rest of the *Book of Church Order*, but (3) they cannot change the meaning of an amendment. These copy edits become an official part of the *Book of Church Order* and can be changed by an amendment at a later Council of Elders.

15.3.5 The confirmation of the members of the Sovereign Grace Court of Appeal

    15.3.5.1 These candidates are drawn from the pool of current Regional Judicial Review Committee members.

    15.3.5.2 The Sovereign Grace Nominating Committee will put forth the most qualified men (see BCO-16.1; BCO-16.2.1).

    15.3.5.3 Each candidate must be individually confirmed by a simple majority of those present and voting in the convened Council of Elders.

    15.3.5.4 See BCO-26 for explanation of the Sovereign Grace Court of Appeal.

15.3.6 Adjudication of charges against a Region (see BCO-26.2.3)

15.3.7 Election of the members of the Executive Committee

15.3.7.1 The candidates are nominated by the Sovereign Grace Nominating Committee and elected by the Council of Elders. The Nominating Committee shall put forward at least twice as many candidates as there are open seats on the Executive Committee.

15.3.7.2 Should any candidate withdraw after selection by the Nominating Committee and before the Council of Elders election, an exception to the 40-day requirement shall be made and the Nominating Committee should seek to fill the slot if possible. If unable to find a replacement the ballot shall simply have a reduced number of candidates. If there are not enough candidates to fill the empty slots, the Executive Committee may appoint members who shall serve until the next election, where they shall need to be elected to continue serving. Terms shall be adjusted to ensure no more than three Executive Committee slots are up for election in each future election.

15.3.7.3 Each candidate must be elected by a simple majority vote of those present and voting at the convened Council of Elders. Run-offs may be necessary.

15.3.8 Confirmation of the Executive Director of the Leadership Team

After the Executive Committee has chosen the Executive Director candidate, he must be confirmed by a simple majority of the Council of Elders.

15.3.9 Changes to the Ordination Standards and Exams

15.3.9.1 Changes to the Ordination Standards and Exams can be proposed by the Leadership Team, the Theology Committee, the Executive Committee or any three members of the Council of Elders.

15.3.9.2 Potential changes must be submitted to the Executive Committee 90 days in advance of the annual Council of Elders meeting in order to give time for the proposed change to be studied and to get it on the Council's agenda.

15.3.9.3 60 days in advance of the Council of Elders meeting, the proposed change must be sent to every member of the Council.

15.3.9.4 The Theology Committee will be charged with the responsibility to study the proposed changes and give their reasoned input at the next Council meeting.

15.3.9.5 The Council of Elders must confirm Ordination Standards and Exams and changes thereto by a three-fourths majority vote of those present and voting.

15.3.9.6 Ordination Standards and Exams must then be affirmed by three-fourths of the Regions.

15.3.10 Affirmation of the Sovereign Grace Yearly Budget

After the Executive Committee has approved a yearly budget, it must be affirmed by a simple majority of the Council of Elders.

15.3.11 Public Statements by the Council of Elders

The Council of Elders may, as a body, make public statements on any issue that it wishes to speak to, issue opinions, or publicly censure or commend any individual person, church, denomination, public official, or human government that it deems advisable and for the good of our ecclesiastical union. Public statements on behalf of the Council of Elders must be approved by no less than a two-thirds majority vote of the elders present and voting in a Council of Elders meeting.

15.4 Procedures for Council of Elders Meetings

15.4.1 New Business Motions

15.4.1.1 A New Business Motion is any motion that requires the Council of Elders to take any substantive decisions or actions, such as, but not limited to, the appropriation of funds not already in the budget, the formation of new committees, the issuing of opinions and public statements on behalf of the Council of Elders, public censures, and commendations.

15.4.1.2 Any New Business Motion must be submitted to the Executive Committee 40 days prior to the Council of Elders meeting. This will give the Executive Committee 10 days to review such a motion, if necessary refer it to an appropriate existing committee, and/or to interact with the elder making the motion with its recommendation. The new motion will, either in its original form or with modifications *agreed to by the elder making the motion*, be sent to every Council of Elders member 30 days prior to the Council of Elders meeting. This will give each Council of Elders member the opportunity to give due consideration to the motion and to discuss it with the other elders in his church.

15.4.1.3 Exception: Procedural motions on business items are not subject to this procedure. Procedural motions include, but are not limited to (1) motions concerning points of order, (2) motions to open or close debates, (3) motions to table business items to a future meeting, (4) motions to refer an item to a committee for further study, and (5) changes made to the motion as a result of dialogue and debate by the Council of Elders.

15.4.1.4 Exception: It is also allowable for the Council of Elders to suspend its own requirement for notice for new business motions *if there is a two-thirds majority vote of the Council of Elders*.

15.4.2 Rules of Order for Council of Elders Meetings

15.4.2.1 All Council of Elders meetings will be governed by the Sovereign Grace *Book of Church Order* and the most recent edition of *The Modern Rules of Order* except where *The Modern Rules of Order* is inconsistent with the Sovereign Grace *Book of Church Order*.

15.4.2.2 While in session, the Council of Elders may suspend a *Book of Church Order* procedural rule with a two-thirds majority vote in order to conduct necessary business.

15.4.3 Rules Committee

15.4.3.1 The Polity Committee shall supply three of its members to serve as the standing Rules Committee. The Rules Committee will give rulings on any questions concerning what the *Book of Church Order* stipulates, allows, or prohibits during Council of Elders meetings if a point of order is made during the meeting. A ruling of the Rules Committee may be appealed by any member of the Council of Elders and voted on by the Council.

15.4.3.2 The Polity Committee shall determine beforehand which of its members serve at each Council of Elders meeting.

15.4.4 Others Participating in Council of Elders but not Voting

Executive Committee Members, Leadership Team Members, Theology Committee, Polity Committee, Court of Appeals, and Regional Leaders who are not Council of Elders delegates from their local church may participate in the Council of Elders by making statements or asking questions but may not vote or make motions from the floor.

15.4.5 Minutes for the Council of Elders and Its Committees

Minutes must be taken at all official business meetings of the Council of Elders and of its attendant committees (including the Executive Committee) and of the Sovereign Grace Court of Appeals. These need not be word-for-word transcripts, but they should include at least (1) the official agenda, (2) decisions made and votes taken, (3) a summary of the major points brought up in debate or discussion, and (4) any statement, especially of dissent or protest, that a member requests be included in the minutes. Council of Elders minutes will be approved by the Executive Committee. Minutes for other committee meetings will be approved by the members of the respective committee. All minutes will be responsibly archived.

16 Sovereign Grace Nominating Committee

16.1 Purpose

The Sovereign Grace Nominating Committee will be established to put forth godly and experienced candidates to serve in key functions for the governance of Sovereign Grace churches. Its composition will reflect a broad range of representation (weighted toward Regional Leaders but including centralized leadership) while seeking the most qualified members possible who are most able to discern the best candidates for the positions it nominates. Its function is to bring wisdom, experience, and expertise to the selection of key positions within Sovereign Grace.

16.2 The Responsibilities of the Nominating Committee

16.2.1 The Nominating Committee will nominate members of the Regional Judicial Review Committees to serve on the Sovereign Grace Court of Appeal (BCO-26.1), subject to the affirmation of the Council of Elders by simple majority vote.

16.2.2 The Nominating Committee will nominate two or more qualified Sovereign Grace elders to fill each vacant seat on the Executive Committee. From among these candidates, the Council of Elders will elect the requisite number of Executive Committee members. Each candidate must receive the support of at least a simple majority of those present and voting. Run-offs may be necessary (see BCO-17.1.4).

16.2.3 Should the Council of Elders see fit to create other committees, their members shall be nominated by the Nominating Committee and individually confirmed by a simple majority vote of the Council of Elders (cf. BCO-15.3.1).

16.3 The Members of the Nominating Committee

16.3.1 Composition

The Sovereign Grace Nominating Committee will consist of five representatives of the Regional Leaders, one representative of the existing Executive Committee, and one representative of the Leadership Team. The Regional Leaders will select five of their own members to serve, the Leadership Team will select one of its own members to serve, and the Executive Committee will select one of its own members to serve on the Nominating Committee. This particular mixture of numbers lends weight to the influence of the Regional Leaders while providing the insight and counsel a member of the Executive Committee and Leadership Team can bring.

16.3.2 Term: The members of the Nominating Committee will serve three-year terms.

16.3.3 The Nominating Committee must have its full complement of members 60 days prior to the election of the members of the Executive Committee and Sovereign Grace Court of Appeal. To ensure this, it is the responsibility of the Executive Committee, the Leadership Team, and the Regional Leaders to supply their representatives to the Nominating Committee in a timely manner.

17 The Executive Committee of the Council of Elders

The Executive Committee exists as an extension of the Council of Elders. Its primary responsibility is oversight of the Leadership Team on behalf of the Council of Elders. Its specific responsibilities are strictly limited to those listed in BCO-17.2.

17.1 The Selection of the members of the Executive Committee

17.1.1 The Executive Committee will consist of nine members.

17.1.2 The Nominating Committee will nominate two or more candidates for each open seat on the Executive Committee.

17.1.3 An Executive Committee candidate must be a Sovereign Grace pastor in good standing and recommended by the elders of his church.

17.1.4 The Council of Elders will elect the members of the Executive Committee from the slate of candidates put forward by the Nominating Committee (cf. BCO-16.2.2). A candidate must have the support of a simple majority of the votes cast by the Council of Elders. If necessary, run-offs shall be held until the available seats on the Executive Committee are thus filled.

17.2 The Executive Committee will have the following responsibilities:

17.2.1 To insure that the Leadership Team and its officers are acting in accordance with the mission and core values of the Sovereign Grace churches;

17.2.2 To appoint and evaluate the Leadership Team;

17.2.3 To steward the financial assets of Sovereign Grace;

17.2.4 To approve the annual budget of Sovereign Grace;

17.2.5 To determine the responsibilities of the Leadership Team;

17.2.6 To select a member to serve on the Nominating Committee;

17.2.7 To keep current and maintain the Sovereign Grace Articles of Incorporation and corporate bylaws and keep them consistent with our *Book of Church Order*;

17.2.8 To select a chairman from among its members to facilitate decision-making, lead discussions, and serve as a point of contact for whole committee.

17.3 Terms of Executive Committee Members

17.3.1 Once elected and affirmed, an Executive Committee member will serve a four-year term.

17.3.2 There will be no term limits.

17.3.3 The secretary of the Executive Committee will keep accurate records of the terms of each Committee member and give adequate notice to the Nominating Committee and the Council of Elders of expiring terms.

18 Leadership Team

18.1 Definition and Rationale

Leadership is a gift from the Lord and is to be honored and cultivated in our ecclesiastical union. The Leadership Team is appointed and empowered from our Council of Elders and Executive Committee for the expressed purpose of providing leadership that is Biblical, humble, faith-filled, discerning, and gospel-centered.

Within Sovereign Grace, the Leadership Team constitutes men that the churches of Sovereign Grace recognize and designate for specialized tasks, such as leadership in mission, pastoral training, and administrative functions for the wider ecclesiastical body.

Members of the Leadership Team do not occupy a special office in addition to that of an elder but rather are elders (or men of similar qualification) whose gifting for these types of broader leadership is recognized by other elders. As such, the Leadership Team emerges from our churches and is accountable to the elders of Sovereign Grace through their representatives on the Executive Committee. It is, in essence, a ministry arm of our elders, providing specialized leadership and coordination in aspects of our broader mission.

The Leadership Team exists to help facilitate and ensure proper and efficient execution of our shared mission. Their leadership augments our efficiency while supporting the expressed authority of the Sovereign Grace elders and their representatives.

18.2 Qualifications

Specific qualifications will be determined by the Executive Committee. At a minimum, a Leadership Team member should be a member of a Sovereign Grace church and, therefore, accountable to its eldership for his moral integrity. We envision certain members of the Leadership Team (e.g., Executive Director, Director of Church Development) being elders in their respective local church due to their specific function.

18.3 Leadership Team Responsibilities

18.3.1 The Mandate

To facilitate and lead as a team in executing the central aspects of our mission according to the values of Sovereign Grace under the oversight of the Executive Committee in partnership with our churches, their elders, and the Regional Leaders. The following list represents the primary responsibilities of the Leadership Team but is not intended to be an exhaustive description of their actions. Members of the Leadership Team must comply with what the *Book of Church Order* explicitly mandates and refrain from what it explicitly forbids, while operating in biblical wisdom in all other matters.

    18.3.1.1   Specifically, to do all that is delegated to them by the Executive Committee and under its oversight.

    18.3.1.2   These responsibilities can be conceived of under the headings of mission, doctrine, values, and partnership.

18.3.2   With Respect to the Mission:

    18.3.2.1   In cooperation with the Regional Assemblies, to train church planters and coordinate the planting of new churches;

    18.3.2.2   In cooperation with Regional Leaders, to coordinate the care of Sovereign Grace pastors and churches;

    18.3.2.3   In cooperation with the Regions, to facilitate and administrate global missions;

    18.3.2.4   In cooperation with the Regions, to identify, investigate, approve, and facilitate all church adoptions.

18.3.3   With Respect to our Doctrine and Values:

    18.3.3.1   To provide leadership, theological instruction, and pastoral care to the Sovereign Grace Pastors College;

    18.3.3.2   To provide continuing theological and pastoral instruction to Sovereign Grace pastors;

    18.3.3.3   In conjunction with the Theology Committee, the Leadership Team develops and maintains Sovereign Grace Ordination Standards and Examinations;

    18.3.3.4   In conjunction with the Council of Elders, to steward the Sovereign Grace *Statement of Faith*;

    18.3.3.5   To help the pastors of Sovereign Grace process controversies and current events with wisdom and biblical discernment.

18.3.4   With Respect to our Partnership:

    18.3.4.1   To develop resources for ministry within Sovereign Grace;

    18.3.4.2   To plan and execute Sovereign Grace conferences;

    18.3.4.3   To coordinate activities and ministry between Regions;

    18.3.4.4   To communicate, as they deem necessary, on behalf of Sovereign Grace Churches to the broader world in regard to the shared values, beliefs, policies, and standards of Sovereign Grace Churches contained in the *Statement of Faith* and the *Book of Church Order*. They may also communicate, concerning matters such as our practices, history, operations, pastoral conduct, and denominational priorities as well as current or emerging needs;

    18.3.4.5   To facilitate communication and cooperation among the churches and leaders within Sovereign Grace;

18.3.4.6 Under the oversight of the Executive Committee, to administrate the collection and distribution of Sovereign Grace financial resources;

18.3.4.7 To spearhead fundraising;

18.3.4.8 To provide leadership in concert with the Executive Committee when timely actions or statements are needed to serve the churches of Sovereign Grace, and to handle the immediate needs that arise.

18.4 Personnel

The Executive Committee in consultation with the Executive Director determines which positions will comprise the Leadership Team and who will fill these positions. At a minimum, the Leadership Team must include an Executive Director. The rest of the Leadership Team should be staffed sufficiently to fulfill its designated function.

Further, the Executive Committee in consultation with the Executive Director may rename any of the titles of the other leadership team officers except the Executive Director at their discretion. If it does so, any changes to those titles will be made by the Polity Committee in the next edition of the *Book of Church Order* without a formal amendment process.

Should the Executive Committee rename or alter positions presently written into the *Book of Church Order* it is the committee's responsibility to ensure that the Leadership Team will continue to operate in full compliance with the *Book of Church Order* requirements vis-à-vis the Leadership Team.

18.4.1 Executive Director

The Executive Director is to use his leadership gifts to inspire and impart vision to Sovereign Grace, resulting in joyful participation in our shared mission and appreciation of our shared doctrine and values. He is to motivate, encourage and exhort Sovereign Grace to fulfill our shared commitments and warn us against cultural temptations or internal inconsistencies with our doctrine and values.

The Executive Director is the presiding officer of the Leadership Team who answers directly to the Executive Committee. He is a non-voting member of the Executive Committee. He must be an elder in a local Sovereign Grace church. He must be confirmed by a simple majority of the Council of Elders. He is responsible to:

18.4.1.1 Ensure the successful operation of the Leadership Team through strategic planning, support, evaluation, and movement-wide communication;

18.4.1.2 Facilitate successful operation of the polity and mission, movement-wide, through ensuring that the Leadership Team supports and interacts with Regions, Regional Leaders, and globally associated churches;

18.4.1.3 Oversee and support fundraising for Sovereign Grace;

18.4.1.4 Serve as Chair for the Council of Elders, overseeing official meetings and coordinating all its key functions. He may temporarily appoint a Special Chair of his choosing to serve in his stead. Should the Executive Director be unable to appoint a Special Chair when needed, the Executive Committee will appoint one of their choosing;

18.4.1.5 Serve as the authoritative point of contact for all Leadership Team ministry functions;

18.4.1.6 Promote the health and plurality of the Leadership Team to maximize the effectiveness of each director;

18.4.1.7 Report annually to the Council of Elders on the state of the union of Sovereign Grace churches, including a full assessment of and plans for the progress of our mission along with all relevant financial, legal, and statistical data. This report, along with a full financial statement, will be published and made available to all Sovereign Grace elderships.

18.4.2 Director of Church Planting and Mission

Coordinates church planting and church adoptions.

18.4.3 Director of Finance and Administration

Administrates the functions of the Leadership Team, coordinate finances, conferencing, resource distribution, etc.

18.4.4 Director of Church Development

Communicates with the Regional Leaders and coordinates care of all Regions.

18.4.5 Director of Theology and Training

Dean of the Pastors College, chair of the Theology Committee, and facilitates theological training for Sovereign Grace pastors.

18.4.6 Director of Global Missions

Leads our global missions efforts by casting vision, providing theological discernment, and implementing strategic plans in coordination with our global partners. The Director of Global Missions also directs global church planting and adoptions.

18.4.7 Director of Sovereign Grace Music

18.4.8 Director of Emerging Nations

Coordinates church planting and provides strategic leadership for churches outside of the U.S. who have an interest in formalizing a partnership with Sovereign Grace

18.4.9 With the exception of the Executive Director, any member of the Leadership Team may be terminated from his position by a majority vote of the Executive Committee. Similarly, the Executive Committee may suspend with or without pay any member of the Leadership Team at its sole discretion.

18.4.10 The Executive Director may be suspended with or without pay at the sole discretion of the Executive Committee. However, he may not be permanently removed from his position without the approval of a majority of the Council of Elders. The Council of Elders may reinstate the pay of a suspended Executive Director at its discretion.

18.4.11 Leadership Team Committees and Teams

18.4.11.1 In order to support the functions of the Leadership Team, its members may establish committees or teams.

18.4.11.2 Members of committees or teams do not need to be nominated by any nominating committee. They may be selected by the Leadership Team or its members.

18.4.11.3 Ad hoc committees or teams established by the Leadership Team serve in an advisory and assistant capacity, not in the stead of any member of the Leadership Team, nor can they be empowered with any authority already allocated in the *Book of Church Order*.

19 Partnership Agreements

19.1 Partnership Agreement for Provisional Regions[13]

19.1.1 Preamble

The Sovereign Grace churches together voluntarily form a unified ecclesiastical body (Sovereign Grace Churches) to glorify God as an expression of the bride of Christ. The churches share spiritual and material resources for the furtherance of our common mission, under a common government, which guards our fidelity to our common *Statement of Faith* and standards of corporate holiness. A local church (Church Partner) joins itself to the Sovereign Grace Churches when its elders, representing the Church Partner, enter into this Partnership Agreement with Sovereign Grace Churches, represented by its Executive Director, and its Regional Assembly of Elders, represented by the Regional Leader of the provisional region.

19.1.2 The Partnership Commitments

19.1.2.1 The Commitments of the Regional Assembly of Elders

The Regional Assembly of Elders recognizes that the terms and conditions of this Partnership Agreement are an integral part of The *Book of Church Order* of the Sovereign Grace Churches (BCO), and promises to uphold its commitments in the *Book of Church Order* among which are 1) to responsibly steward its role in the examination and approval of elder candidates for ordination in the Church Partner; 2) to pursue justice, righteousness, and holiness as it adjudicates conflicts involving the Church Partner; 3) to coordinate and support church planting and outreach within the Region; and 4) to care for the Church Partner and her elders in time of need. Any aspects of the *Book of Church Order* that cannot be upheld because of national or local requirements and limitations shall be specified, documented and authorized by the Sovereign Grace Churches Leadership Team in cooperation with the Church Partner. The document containing the exceptions must be approved by a simple majority of the Council of Elders. No exceptions to the *Statement of Faith* will be granted.

---

[13] This Partnership Agreement is for "Church Partners" without a current national or region-specific Partnership Agreement who nevertheless wish to confirm their full partnership with Sovereign Grace. Region-specific agreements begin at BCO-19.2 with the Partnership Agreement for United States Regions. Others will be added as they are written and approved by the Council of Elders.

19.1.2.2 The Commitments of Sovereign Grace Churches

Sovereign Grace Churches, on behalf of the Sovereign Grace Churches Council of Elders (Council of Elders) recognizes that the terms and conditions of this Partnership Agreement are an integral part of the *Book of Church Order* and promises to uphold its commitments in the *Book of Church Order* among which are 1) to steward the *Statement of Faith* by pursuing sound, biblical doctrine that includes Reformed Soteriology and Continuationist Pneumatology; 2) to maintain the *Book of Church Order* and to ensure its consistent implementation throughout all Regions; 3) to provide theological education via the Pastors College and training opportunities to the elders of every Church Partner; 4) to coordinate all Regions in the planting of churches globally as God would grant the resources to do so; and 5) to vigorously maintain and promote all of the unique values of Sovereign Grace Churches including elder governed/led polity, complementarian roles in the home and church, and gospel-centered doctrine and preaching. Any aspects of the *Book of Church Order* that cannot be upheld because of national or local requirements and limitations shall be specified, documented and authorized by the Sovereign Grace Churches Leadership Team in cooperation with the Church Partner. The document containing the exceptions must be approved by a simple majority of the Council of Elders. No exceptions to the *Statement of Faith* will be granted.

19.1.2.3 The Commitments of the Church Partner

The Church Partner recognizes that the terms and conditions of this Partnership Agreement are an integral part of the BCO, and promises to uphold its commitments contained in the *Book of Church Order* among which are 1) to subscribe to the *Statement of Faith* (as articulated in Sections 9 and 13); 2) to submit to the *Book of Church Order* (as articulated in Sections 9 and 13); 3) to actively participate in the Regional Assembly of Elders and Council of Elders; and 4) to actively support the mission and values of Sovereign Grace Churches in spirit, through participation, and by giving financially. Any aspects of the *Book of Church Order* that cannot be upheld because of national or local requirements and limitations shall be specified, documented and authorized by the Sovereign Grace Churches Leadership Team in cooperation with the Church Partner. The document containing the exceptions must be approved by a simple majority of the Council of Elders. No exceptions to the *Statement of Faith* will be granted.

19.1.3 Terms and Conditions of Partnership
    19.1.3.1 Declarations of Intentions
        19.1.3.1.a This Agreement does not constitute a formation of a corporation (whether for profit or not-for-profit), a limited liability company, a charitable trust, a charitable incorporated company, a legal partnership, a joint venture, or any other type of social enterprise or legal entity, an employment-employee relationship, an independent contractor/consultant relationship nor any similar entity as defined by the civil laws of each Party's respective government.
        19.1.3.1.b Each Party's execution of this Agreement does not confer to any other party hereto the legal right to or any interest in such executing party's real property, personal property, intellectual property, employees, or responsibility or liability for such party's debts, claims, or liabilities.
        19.1.3.1.c Entering into this Agreement is entirely voluntary, which means that nothing herein is intended to prevent any Church Partner from leaving, as described in the *Book of Church Order*.
        19.1.3.1.d Notwithstanding this Agreement, the Church Partner shall continue to be solely responsible to fulfill its corporate purposes, as currently described by its governing documents, and to operate in a manner consistent with its status as Church within its locale.
    19.1.3.2 Partnership Giving Plan
        19.1.3.2.a To fund this partnership in church planting, church development, and global mission efforts, each Church Partner commits to a goal of giving 10% of their annual general (non-designated) fund giving. The particular distribution of this money will be determined by the Sovereign Grace Churches Leadership Team in cooperation with the church partner and any provisional region.
        19.1.3.2.b The Church Partner agrees to share fairly and proportionally in the expenses of any Regional Assembly of Elders events and activities in which its elders participate, or to make other arrangements in collaboration with, and with the consent of, the other Church Partners.
    19.1.3.3 Intellectual Property
        19.1.3.3.a The Church Partner agrees to respect copyright ownership of all materials owned and/or licensed by

Sovereign Grace Churches and to abide by its policies and procedures for using such materials.

19.1.3.3.b The Church Partner acknowledges that the **Sovereign Grace®** name and logo are trademarks owned by Sovereign Grace Churches. Sovereign Grace Churches grants to each Church Partner a nonexclusive license to use the **Sovereign Grace®** name and logo to identify its affiliation with Sovereign Grace Churches.

19.1.3.4 Indemnification

19.1.3.4.a Each Church Partner will be responsible for determining its own risk management strategy, including maintaining appropriate levels of insurance coverage, implementing a safe and prudent child protection policy, and other measures.

19.1.3.4.b As independent and autonomously governed entities, each Church Partner acknowledges and understands it is solely responsible for all respective claims, loss, damage, liability, or expenses occasioned or claimed by reason of acts or neglects of its own employees, independent contractors, invitees, or guests.

19.1.4 Signature Document

    19.1.4.1 The Executive Director, on behalf of Sovereign Grace Churches

I, the undersigned Executive Director of Sovereign Grace Churches, having prayerfully and soberly considered this Partnership Agreement, with God as witness, representing the Council of Elders, enter into it assuming all of the responsibilities and privileges described therein.

Printed Name:_____

Signature:_____,
Executive Director, Sovereign Grace Churches

Date:_____

    19.1.4.2 The Regional Leader, on behalf of the Regional Assembly of Elders

I, the undersigned Regional Leader, having prayerfully and soberly considered this Partnership Agreement, with God as witness, representing all the elders in the Region enter into it assuming all of the responsibilities and privileges described herein.

Sovereign Grace Region:_____

Printed Name: _____

Signature:_____,
Regional Leader

Date:_____

19.1.4.3 The Local Elders, on behalf of the Church Partner

We, the current undersigned elders, having prayerfully and soberly considered this Partnership Agreement, with God as witness, enter into it, on behalf of the Church Partner, assuming all of the responsibilities and privileges described herein.

Church Name:_____

City/State:_____

Printed Name:_____   Printed Name:_____

Signature:_____Date:_____   Signature:_____Date:_____

Printed Name:_____   Printed Name:_____

Signature:_____Date:_____   Signature:_____Date:_____

Printed Name:_____   Printed Name:_____

Signature:_____Date:_____   Signature:_____Date:_____

Printed Name:_____   Printed Name:_____

Signature:_____Date:_____   Signature:_____Date:_____

19.2 Partnership Agreement for United States Regions

19.2.1 Preamble

The Sovereign Grace churches together voluntarily form a unified ecclesiastical body (Sovereign Grace Churches) to glorify God as an expression of the bride of Christ. The churches share spiritual and material resources for the furtherance of our common mission, under a common government, which guards our fidelity to our common *Statement of Faith* and standards of corporate holiness. A local church (Church Partner) joins itself to the Sovereign Grace Churches when its elders, representing the Church Partner, enter into this Partnership Agreement with Sovereign Grace Churches, represented by its Executive Director, and its Regional Assembly of Elders, represented by the Regional Leader.

19.2.2 The Partnership Commitments

19.2.2.1 The Commitments of the Regional Assembly of Elders

The Regional Assembly of Elders recognizes that the terms and conditions of this Partnership Agreement are an integral part of *The Book of Church Order of the Sovereign Grace Churches* (BCO), and promises to uphold its commitments in the *Book of Church Order* among which are 1) to responsibly steward its role in the examination and approval of elder candidates for ordination in the Church Partner, 2) to pursue justice, righteousness, and holiness as it adjudicates conflicts involving the Church Partner, 3) to coordinate and support church planting and outreach within the Region, and 4) to care for the Church Partner and her elders in time of need.

19.2.2.2 The Commitments of Sovereign Grace Churches

Sovereign Grace Churches, on behalf of the Sovereign Grace Churches Council of Elders (Council of Elders) recognizes that the terms and conditions of this Partnership Agreement are an integral part of the *Book of Church Order* and promises to uphold its commitments in the *Book of Church Order* among which are 1) to steward the *Statement of Faith* by pursuing sound, biblical doctrine that includes Reformed Soteriology and Continuationist Pneumatology; 2) to maintain the *Book of Church Order* and to ensure its consistent implementation throughout all Regions; 3) to provide theological education via the Pastors College and training opportunities to the elders of every Church Partner; 4) to coordinate all Regions in the planting of churches globally as God would grant the resources to do so; and 5) to vigorously maintain and promote all of the unique values of

Sovereign Grace Churches including elder governed/led polity, complementarian roles in the home and church, and gospel-centered doctrine and preaching.

19.2.2.3 The Commitments of the Church Partner

The Church Partner recognizes that the terms and conditions of this Partnership Agreement are an integral part of the *Book of Church Order*, and promises to uphold its commitments contained in the *Book of Church Order* among which are 1) to subscribe to the *Statement of Faith* (as articulated in Sections 9 and 13); 2) to submit to the *Book of Church Order* (as articulated in Sections 9 and 13); 3) to actively participate in the Regional Assembly of Elders and Council of Elders; and 4) to actively support the mission and values of Sovereign Grace Churches in spirit, through participation, and by giving financially.

19.2.3 Terms and Conditions of Partnership

19.2.3.1 Declarations of Intentions

19.2.3.1.a This Agreement does not constitute a formation of a corporation (whether for profit or not-for-profit), a limited liability company, a legal partnership, a joint venture, or any other type of legal entity, an employment-employee relationship, or an independent contractor/consultant relationship.

19.2.3.1.b Each Party's execution of this Agreement does not confer to any other party hereto the legal right to or any interest in such executing party's real property, personal property, intellectual property, employees, or responsibility or liability for such party's debts, claims, or liabilities.

19.2.3.1.c Entering into this Agreement is entirely voluntary, which means that nothing herein is intended to prevent any Church Partner from leaving, as described in the *Book of Church Order*.

19.2.3.1.d Notwithstanding this Agreement, the Church Partner shall continue to be solely responsible to fulfill its corporate purposes, as currently described by its governing documents, and to operate in a manner consistent with its status as a tax-exempt nonprofit organization under Section 501(c)(3) of the Internal Revenue Code.

19.2.3.1.e This Agreement recognizes the independence of the Church of Jesus Christ from the control of the government as provided in the First Amendment of the Constitution of the United States because it reflects the Church Partner's sincerely-held beliefs and practices contained in the Bible and in the *Book of Church Order* with respect to a regional collaboration with other local churches united in the mission of Sovereign Grace.

19.2.3.1.f For Church Partners outside the United States who, for legal and/or cultural reasons, are not able to sign this Partnership Agreement, the Leadership Team will propose a modified Partnership Agreement to be included in Section 19 of the *Book of Church Order* in accordance with BCO-15.3.3 (approval of changes to the *Book of Church Order*).

19.2.3.2 Partnership Giving Plan

19.2.3.2.a To fund this partnership in church planting, church development, and global mission efforts, each Church Partner commits to a goal of giving 10% of their annual general (non-designated) fund giving. Unless or until the Council of Elders modifies these distribution percentages, the annual giving will be allocated as follows: the first 5% will support our central functions, and the second 5% will support the region of the member church.

19.2.3.2.b The Church Partner agrees to share fairly and proportionally in the expenses of any Regional Assembly of Elders events and activities in which its elders participate, or to make other arrangements in collaboration with, and with the consent of, the other Church Partners.

19.2.3.3 Intellectual Property

19.2.3.3.a The Church Partner agrees to respect copyright ownership of all materials owned and/or licensed by Sovereign Grace Churches and to abide by its policies and procedures for using such materials.

19.2.3.3.b The Church Partner acknowledges that the **Sovereign Grace**® name and logo are trademarks owned by Sovereign Grace Churches. Sovereign Grace Churches grants to each Church Partner a nonexclusive license to use the **Sovereign Grace**® name and logo to identify its affiliation with Sovereign Grace Churches.

19.2.3.4 Indemnification

19.2.3.4.a Each Church Partner will be responsible for determining its own risk management strategy, including maintaining appropriate levels of insurance coverage, implementing a safe and prudent child protection policy, and other measures.

19.2.3.4.b   As independent and autonomously governed entities, each Church Partner acknowledges and understands it is solely responsible for all respective claims, loss, damage, liability, or expenses occasioned or claimed by reason of acts or neglects of its own employees, independent contractors, invitees, or guests.

19.2.4   Signature Document

19.2.4.1   The Executive Director, on behalf of Sovereign Grace Churches

I, the undersigned Executive Director of Sovereign Grace Churches, having prayerfully and soberly considered this Partnership Agreement, with God as witness, representing the Council of Elders, enter into it assuming all of the responsibilities and privileges described therein.

Printed Name:_____

Signature:_____,
Executive Director, Sovereign Grace Churches

Date:_____

19.2.4.2   The Regional Leader, on behalf of the Regional Assembly of Elders

I, the undersigned Regional Leader, having prayerfully and soberly considered this Partnership Agreement, with God as witness, representing all the elders in the Region enter into it assuming all of the responsibilities and privileges described herein.

Sovereign Grace Region:_____

Printed Name: _____

Signature:_____,
Regional Leader

Date:_____

19.2.4.3 The Local Elders, on behalf of the Church Partner

We, the current undersigned elders, having prayerfully and soberly considered this Partnership Agreement, with God as witness, enter into it, on behalf of the Church Partner, assuming all of the responsibilities and privileges described herein.

Church Name:_____

City/State:_____

Printed Name:_____	Printed Name:_____
Signature:_____ Date:_____	Signature:_____ Date:_____
Printed Name:_____	Printed Name:_____
Signature:_____ Date:_____	Signature:_____ Date:_____
Printed Name:_____	Printed Name:_____
Signature:_____ Date:_____	Signature:_____ Date:_____
Printed Name:_____	Printed Name:_____
Signature:_____ Date:_____	Signature:_____ Date:_____
Printed Name:_____	Printed Name:_____
Signature:_____ Date:_____	Signature:_____ Date:_____

19.3 Partnership for Historic Sovereign Grace Churches Outside the United States without a Current Partnership Agreement

All historic Sovereign Grace churches that previously signed the Letter of Intent/Pledge of Membership in 2013, according to the stipulations outlined in BCO-19 (2nd Ed.), shall remain, along with all their ordained elders, members in good standing in Sovereign Grace Churches. This includes the following: (1) sending delegates to the Council of Elders, (2) participating in Sovereign Grace committees, and (3) sharing in the benefits and commitments of a Sovereign Grace church as facilitated by the Leadership Team.

20 Process of Separation for a Local Church from Sovereign Grace

20.1 General Principles

20.1.1 We are an ecclesiastical union. No separation of such a union should be taken lightly or unadvisedly, but soberly, carefully, and only in light of strong reasons of conscience or compatibility, and then only after earnest efforts have been made to preserve our unity in the Spirit (cf. BCO-1.10).

20.1.2 There may arise by necessity a time in which a local church for reason of a change of doctrine or other unforeseen reasons can no longer in good faith continue to be part of the Sovereign Grace churches.

20.1.3 Upon separation, Sovereign Grace has no right to the property of a local church, and the local church has no right to the property of Sovereign Grace, except as qualified below.

20.1.4 Beginning with the adoption of this *Sovereign Grace Book of Church Order*, any local church planted with the financial assistance of Sovereign Grace which separates from Sovereign Grace within five years of receiving a church plant grant must repay a prorated amount of the financial assistance that it received. Churches leaving in less than one year must repay 100%, churches leaving in less than two years must repay 80%, churches leaving in less than three years must repay 60%, churches leaving in less than four years must repay 40%, and churches leaving in less than five years must repay 20%.

20.2 Procedure

The following procedures are outlined as a proper expression of mutual respect and affection and a desire to humbly and carefully address the possibility of separation.

Sovereign Grace's polity gives tangible expression to God's command to pursue doctrinally substantiated unity and love (John 17:20-23) by connecting congregations to a broader ecclesiastical body of affiliated churches. In protecting the reputation of Christ, every church should make a concerted, vigorous, and lasting effort to maintain the unity of the Spirit in the bond of peace, modeling the love of Christ in its given communion of churches, by only withdrawing from such fellowship in exceptional circumstances (BCO-1.10).

Participation in the union of Sovereign Grace churches is ultimately voluntary; any eldership may withdraw a church from Sovereign Grace without legal or financial penalty (except as specified in BCO-20.1.4). The separation procedures below honor the voluntary character of our union but also express its gravity and sobriety.

20.2.1 If a church is considering leaving Sovereign Grace, its elders should contact the Regional Leader and discuss its reasons with him prior to reaching a final decision.

20.2.2 If the local church, through her elders, decides to pursue separation, its elders must notify their Regional Assembly of Elders in writing of their decision of intent to withdraw from Sovereign Grace.

20.2.3 At least 30 days prior to withdrawal, the elders of that local church shall appear before the Judicial Review Committee of their Region in order to give reason(s) for leaving.

20.2.4 The Judicial Review Committee of that Region shall, for the good of the local church and our union, examine in earnest the reasons stated for leaving.

20.2.5 If the Judicial Review Committee accepts the reasons for withdrawal to be valid, then the Judicial Review Committee will recommend to the Regional Assembly of Elders that the local church be commended to the Lord and his grace and freed to leave without censure. Valid reasons include, e.g., a non-heretical disagreement with the Sovereign Grace *Statement of Faith*, a theological inability to submit to the explicit mandates of the Sovereign Grace *Book of Church Order*, or a practical inability to participate in a Regional Assembly of Elders.

20.2.6 If the Judicial Review Committee finds that the eldership of the departing church is (a) heretical (i.e., its errors present a grave and immediate threat to the spiritual welfare of church members), (b) guilty of unrepented scandalous sin, (c) intentionally violating the *Book of Church Order* while maintaining a public appearance of support for it, or (d) has engaged in divisive and destructive behavior (i.e., making or condoning charges against Sovereign Grace members outside of the appropriate church judicatories), then the Judicial Review Committee shall propose to the Regional Assembly of Elders a censure against the eldership stating the reasons why it believes the departure is wrong.

20.2.7 If the Judicial Review Committee finds that an eldership is departing for reasons which do not honor the gravity of ecclesiastical union (cf. BCO-1.10.3), it may propose to the Regional Assembly of Elders the issue of a comment which neither censures nor commends the eldership's decision. Under such circumstances the Judicial Review Committee and the Regional Assembly of Elders are advised to exercise charity and restraint.

20.2.8 After hearing the Judicial Review Committee's proposal, the Regional Assembly of Elders shall determine, by a simple majority vote, whether to commend, censure, or simply comment upon the local church's departure.

20.2.9 A copy of the commendation, censure, or comment will be sent to all elderships in Sovereign Grace for them to communicate to their congregations as they deem appropriate.

20.3 **Dissolving an Existing Church by the Local Elder(s) and the Regional Leader**

When local church elder(s) and the Regional Leader agree that an existing Sovereign Grace church should be dissolved, the Regional Leader or his delegate shall make a recommendation to the Regional Assembly of Elders regarding the potential dissolution of a church within the region.

20.3.1 In order for a local church to be dissolved, the Regional Assembly of Elders must affirm by a two-thirds vote.

20.3.2 In the event a local church is dissolved, the Regional Leader should ensure the Regional Assembly of Elders is extending care to the elder(s) of the dissolving church.

20.3.3 When it has been decided that a local church will be dissolved, the elder(s) should provide a 60-day notice to the members of the local church that intends to dissolve. During this time, the local elders should assist members with their transition to another church.

20.3.4 The dissolution of local church assets must be in accord with the local church bylaws and civil law.

20.3.5 The Region Assembly of Elders and Sovereign Grace Churches have no rights to the assets of a dissolving church unless it is gifted by the local church elder(s) and the dissolution is in accordance with state law and the local church bylaws.

20.4 **Removal of a Church from its Region by its Regional Assembly of Elders**

The Regional Assembly of Elders, under the guidance of the Regional Leader and in consultation with the Sovereign Grace Director of Church Development, may vote to remove a church from the Region. Such a removal may be wise should the church significantly depart from the vision, mission, values, or practices of Sovereign Grace Churches. Removal involving heterodoxy or scandalous sin is covered by the process mandated in BCO-25.2.10.5.a.

20.4.1 The Process

The Regional Leader must appoint two elders from the Regional Assembly of Elders to investigate and make assessment of the church. Their assessment must be shared with the church's elder(s) and opportunity given for the church to make appropriate changes. Should sufficient change not occur, the assessing elders shall make recommendation to the Regional Assembly of Elders to remove the church. Removal would require a three-fourths majority vote of the Regional Assembly of Elders. The Regional Assembly of Elders must give a written basis for its decision.

20.4.2 Appeal by the Local Church

The removed church may appeal this decision to the Sovereign Grace Council of Elders at its next regularly scheduled annual meeting. Each party must present their position in writing to the Council of Elders representatives 30 days prior to the Council of Elders Meeting. The Council members may ask question of the parties. A two-thirds majority vote shall be required for the Council of Elders to overrule the decision of the Regional Assembly of Elders.

PART FOUR: Rules of Discipline

21 Principles of Discipline

21.1 The Context

Delineating church discipline procedures is necessary to ensure that when serious sin and controversies affect our churches, we have clear and consistent biblical principles and subsequent practices in place. Certainly the life of our churches is not derived from the following procedures. The length of this section is not a function of the importance of discipline in the overall life of the church but the necessity of specifically spelling out detailed procedures to best serve our churches, our people, and our elders. Moreover, this section reflects Sovereign Grace's ecclesiastical standards, which are separate from civil laws. This section assumes that the laws of all relevant civil authorities apply and is in no way intended to supersede or counteract such laws.

21.2 The Command

The command and authority to exercise church discipline is given by Christ to the church in Matthew 18:15-22, 1 Corinthians 5, and 1 Timothy 5:19-21.

21.3 The Purpose of Discipline

The purpose of discipline is to promote the glory of Christ, the purity of the church, and the restoration of the sinner.

Holiness is a high priority for all Sovereign Grace churches because the church is a representation and expression of the holiness of God (Rev. 4:8). 1 Peter 2:9-10 explains that the church is "a chosen race, a royal priesthood, a holy nation, a people for his own possession." Likewise, Jesus prefaces his prayer for unity with a petition that God would sanctify his people through the truth of his Word (John 17:17). Unity within the body is to be sought, but never at cost to our holiness. The pursuit and standards of holiness are commanded for all members and especially the leaders of Christ's church.

When discipline involves judicial action against an elder, discipline is for the purpose of publicly rebuking sin, eradicating scandal, protecting the doctrinal and ethical purity of the body, restoring the offender, and defending the reputation of Jesus Christ.

21.4 The Spirit of Discipline

Discipline should be carried out in a spirit of love and impartiality between brothers, pursuing the glory of God above all else. Christ commands the church and its officers to promote the welfare and purity of its members. Discipline is a power given by Christ to the church for this purpose and should not be implemented in a vindictive spirit. The goal of any disciplinary action is one of merciful reclamation and repentance. To this end, discipline serves to protect and promote godliness in the body according to the standards of holiness set down in Scripture (1 Tim. 4:7; 1 Cor. 5:11-13).

21.5 The Name and Reputation of the Elder Protected

Our good name is to be valued, and we are to protect the reputation of others. The Bible tells us that "a good name is to be chosen rather than great riches" (Prov. 22:1), and thus our duty to love others implies that we will also protect their name. This means that sins of slander, gossip, divisiveness, and certain expressions of anger must not be tolerated among the people of God. When the good name of an elder is destroyed, it becomes virtually impossible for the elder to fulfill his office. The process detailed below is meant to balance the proper handling of charges against an elder with the obligation of the church to protect his reputation.

21.6 Peers Able to Judge

The Bible assumes that people are able to judge their peers (1 Cor. 5:12-13; 6:2), and thus there is no need to look beyond the elders of Sovereign Grace, first locally and then extra-locally (whichever is more relevant for the situation), for an objective third-party.

Exodus 18:17-23 describes Moses appointing judges to oversee cases in the nation of Israel. From these passages, we see that impartiality is possible among our peers. Paul likewise assumes that matters can be handled wisely and impartially within the church. Therefore, we are not required to go outside the elders of Sovereign Grace to find men who will be able to judge righteously. So while gathering counsel from third parties is allowable and may at times be commendable, Sovereign Grace reserves the right and authority to adjudicate matters between its members and its elders itself.

21.7 The Process

All adjudications shall proceed according to the *Rules of Procedure for Adjudications* (cf. BCO-15.3.1.3).

22 Discipline in the Local Church

22.1 Original Jurisdiction

The eldership of a local church has jurisdiction over all who are considered members of said church. Original jurisdiction over an elder belongs:

- *First* to the eldership with which he serves,
- *Second* to the Regional Assembly of Elders, whose authority is represented by the Judicial Review Committee, and
- *Third* to the Sovereign Grace Court of Appeal.

This means:

22.1.1 Charges must first be leveled against an elder or member in the context of his local eldership. All subsequent appeals will be made following the chain of original jurisdiction.

22.1.2 If one or more elders bring charges against another elder of their local church, the accusing elders are automatically recused from presiding in judgment on the charge. Any other member of that eldership who cannot impartially hear the case must also recuse himself. If the defendant or the plaintiff believes that any of the elders ought to be recused, they may appeal to the Regional Judicial Review Committee who will rule on the matter. If, after recusals, there are only one or two members of the local eldership who can preside over the case, then the Regional Judicial Review Committee shall supply from among its own members enough elders so that three men preside over the case. The elders who preside over a case at the local church level shall be referred to as the Panel. If, after recusals, no member of the local eldership is available to serve on a Panel, then the Regional Judicial Review Committee shall assume jurisdiction.

22.1.3 If an eldership refuses to hear charges of a doctrinal or publicly scandalous nature and two other elderships file charges with the Regional Judicial Review Committee, the Regional Judicial Review Committee shall assume jurisdiction.

22.1.4 If the Judicial Review Committee with jurisdiction over an elder refuses to hear charges of a doctrinal or publicly scandalous nature and two other Regional Assemblies of Elders file charges with the Sovereign Grace Court of Appeal, the Sovereign Grace Court of Appeal will pick up jurisdiction.

22.2 Local Elders Responsible to Instruct and Lead in this Practice

Local elders have primary responsibility to instruct and lead the congregation in the practice of church discipline and biblical peacemaking. All individuals involved in a disciplinary process should heed the instructions of Galatians 6:1: "Brothers, if anyone is caught in any transgression, you who are spiritual should restore him in a spirit of gentleness. Keep watch on yourself, lest you too be tempted."

23 Discipline of a Church Member

23.1 Principles of Church Discipline in a Local Church

The members of a local church belong to the bride of Christ and as such are to be held accountable for being faithful representatives of Christ on earth. Members are subject to Christ and his Word and, by extension, to the officers he has appointed to lead his Church. As such, they are under the leadership and care of their local elders, who serve as under-shepherds of Christ and will be held accountable for all they teach and do.

Members are subject to the practice of discipline laid out in Matthew 18:15-22 and 1 Corinthians 5, under the elders' leadership. Believers have a responsibility to hold each other accountable for the biblical fidelity of their doctrine and deeds and to admonish each other when they stray. The purpose of this is the merciful restoration of a brother from drift, grievous doctrinal error, or unrepentant sin. The sole standard for judging an offense worthy of discipline is that it is contrary to the Word of God. Sins requiring excommunication are behavioral, serious, and unrepentant. These include but are not limited to: gross sexual immorality, teaching false doctrine, divisiveness, convicted criminal activity, and financial impropriety.

The steps of Matthew 18 should be followed carefully and privacy protected. The initial steps are both informal and gradual. The discipline is formalized if the elders uphold the veracity of the charge(s) and the person continues in unrepentance. If, in due course, the member remains in sin and is resistant to the appeals of the elders, the elders must tell it to the church, so that the church may call the member to repent. If the member persists in sin after the church has called for repentance, he/she should be excommunicated from the church.

However, the goal of any disciplinary action is one of merciful reclamation and repentance. Ultimately, the process of discipline does not conclude with excommunication but should always leave room for future repentance and restoration. The responsibility to receive, excommunicate, and restore church members belongs to the church as a whole (Matt. 18:18-20), but it is specifically given to the church's governing officers to exercise in leadership of the congregation (Matt. 16:18-19; John 20:23; 1 Cor. 4:14-5:13; 2 Cor. 13:1-4). In addition to a full array of other mutual responsibilities (e.g., love, encouragement, care, etc.), congregants are obliged to lovingly confront one another for impenitent sin (Matt. 18:15-16). The elders (as governing officers) are authorized to hear such charges and render a verdict which they pronounce on behalf of the whole church and in its presence, in the name and power of Jesus Christ, as a corporate appeal for the sinner to repent (Matt. 18:17, 20; 1 Cor. 4:19-21; 5:4-5). Congregants have the duty to carry out the discipline of an excommunicated person by treating them as an unbeliever (1 Cor. 5:9-13; 2 Cor. 2:6; 2 Thess. 3:6, 14-15). The elders also decide when to readmit the penitent to the fellowship of the church (2 Cor. 2:6-8).

It is the duty of the congregants to forgive, comfort, and reaffirm their love for such a one (2 Cor. 2:7-8).

23.2 Appealing an Excommunication

23.2.1 A disciplined member may appeal the elders' decision and the church's action to their Regional Judicial Review Committee. The Regional Judicial Review Committee is required to hear the appeal of any excommunicated church member; the Committee may not decline to take up the case. It is the responsibility of the local eldership to communicate to an excommunicated member the right to appeal. An appeal must be made within 30 days of being notified by the elders of their excommunication and right to appeal.

23.2.2 The Regional Judicial Review Committee may not reverse the decision of the local eldership, but they may recommend that the eldership reverse or reconsider its decision.

23.2.3 If the Regional Judicial Review Committee does not recommend a reversal or reconsideration of the original excommunication, the excommunicated member may appeal to the Sovereign Grace Court of Appeal, but the Sovereign Grace Court of Appeal is not obliged to hear the case.

23.2.4 If the Regional Judicial Review Committee recommends that the eldership reverse or reconsider the excommunication, the local eldership may appeal the decision to the Sovereign Grace Court of Appeal. Otherwise, if the local eldership does not reverse or reconsider the excommunication, the Regional Judicial Review Committee may censure the local eldership.

24 Discipline of an Elder

All Sovereign Grace churches will agree to a shared grievance policy for bringing charges against an elder, according to the process in 1 Timothy 5:19-21:

> *Do not admit a charge against an elder except on the evidence of two or three witnesses. [20]As for those who persist in sin, rebuke them in the presence of all, so that the rest may stand in fear. [21]In the presence of God and of Christ Jesus and of the elect angels I charge you to keep these rules without prejudging, doing nothing from partiality.*

First, we should note that Paul is addressing Timothy, a partner in extra-local ministry. The main verbs ("Do not admit [*paradechou*]," "rebuke [*elegche*]," "keep [*phulaxēs*] these things") are second-person singular verbs directed specifically at Timothy. We see this as establishing the precedent that the right authorities to hear an accusation are the governing officers of the church.

Second, we are not to "admit a charge against an elder" without just cause (v. 19). Not all accusations are to be "admitted." Some can be refused as being personal matters to be handled according to basic principles of forgiveness and reconciliation (or Matthew 18:15-20 if necessary). Some charges can be refused because they are not matters sufficient to merit the censure of an elder or disqualification from office. A charge may also be refused if it appears to be a malicious attempt to harm the elder or the church or is primarily sinfully motivated. A charge is admitted when it relates to the elder's office and is weighty enough to engage in the significant process detailed below.

Third, charges are to include "the evidence of two or three witnesses." The testimony of more than one witness is necessary to establish a charge, as a protection against false and unsubstantiated charges. One person's word is often as good as another's, and therefore no individual is to be declared guilty on the basis of a single testimony. However, this rule should not be used to dismiss cases where the testimony of one person is supported by corroborative evidence, or where one person's direct testimony is supported by the indirect testimony of others (that is, testimony from those who have known the man to act in ways that are in keeping with the charge being brought). Also, there are situations with a single witness which ought not be immediately dismissed but should be further investigated for such evidence. These witnesses can serve several roles. At times they have witnessed the same sin or sinful pattern in the elder. They can also substantiate a lack of repentance in the elder. Witnesses can provide testimony of one kind or another throughout the process. Once the trial is underway, witnesses also help to guarantee a fair and impartial process—protecting both the accuser and the elder.

Fourth, it is "those who persist in sin" (v. 20) who are to be rebuked "in the presence of all, so that the rest may stand in fear." While not detailed here, the implication is that such a public rebuke combined with unrepentant sin would require removal from office. In other words, for most sins, what is of critical importance when considering a public rebuke is that there is *an observed pattern of unrepentance* in the elder.

Fifth, because only the impenitent elder is to receive such a public rebuke, the implication is that an elder who repents of his sin or who is cleared of the charge itself need not receive any public censure.

Sixth, it is possible for a church officer to hear the case of another church officer "without prejudging, doing nothing from partiality" (v. 21). The command to do this implies the ability to do this. Despite the myriad temptations of such a situation, Paul assumes that with a deep awareness of the seriousness of the matter, a man will be able to hear such a case wisely: "In the presence of God and of Christ Jesus and of the elect angels I charge you to keep these rules without prejudging, doing nothing from partiality."

24.1 Gross or Scandalous Sins

The nature of the sin or offense requiring removal from office includes any *gross* or *scandalous* failure to comply with the moral requirements laid out for leaders in Scripture (i.e., the moral standards put forth in 1 Timothy 3:1-8 and Titus 1:5-9). As stated above, the demand of such passages is not perfection. Therefore grounds for removal are <u>patterns</u> of sinful and impenitent behavior, not isolated events. Exceptions to this include behavior that is automatically disqualifying with a single occurrence (e.g., sexual immorality).

Furthermore, any sins that would lead to church discipline (1 Cor. 5:11; Titus 3:10) can also be sufficient grounds for removal from office. These include but are not limited to financial impropriety, convicted criminal activity (Rom. 13:1-4), and sexual immorality.

Should an elder confess to serious sin or even be accused of such sins, either the accused elder or the other local elders will immediately contact both the Regional Leader and the Chairman of the Judicial Review Committee.

Should an elder confess to serious sin, and agree to resign from his position, the local elders should immediately contact the Chairman of the Judicial Review Committee in order for him to appoint a Moderator of Just Cause to review the situation and any *Resignation Agreement* (BCO-9.9) in order to confirm that a trial is not necessary. Should the moderator determine the process and agreement are fair and freely agreed upon, the eldership will follow the guidelines contained in BCO-24.9.4.

24.1.1 An Eldership Suspending an Elder

Should an elder be accused of serious criminal or scandalous sin the remaining elders may, at their own discretion, temporarily suspend the accused elder from his office and its duties with or without pay until an Adjudicatory Panel rules on the matter. In a case where the eldership decides to suspend pay, if the elder is ultimately cleared of the charges, he must receive his withheld pay in full. Two unaccused elders are required to approve this action. If there are not two remaining unaccused elders the Judicial Review Committee will supply a second elder or in the case of a single elder, who is accused, the Judicial Review Committee will supply two. In the situation where there is only one elder and he is the accused, the Regional Assembly will assume responsibility for the care of the church. The Regional Leader will coordinate that care. The financial assets of the church remain under the control of the local church officers or their delegates.

24.2 Bringing a Charge

24.2.1 Definition of Offense:

24.2.1.1 Public offenses are any sins or heterodox beliefs that are publicly and commonly known.

24.2.1.2 Private offenses are those that are known only to one or a select few individuals.

24.2.1.3 Private offenses may or may not be personal. Personal private offenses are those which have brought injury to the individual bringing the charge.

24.2.1.4 Criminal Offenses
In the event that an elder is charged with a crime by civil authorities, the local elders must immediately notify the Chairman of the Regional Judicial Review Committee. The local church's eldership will appoint one of its member elders as Moderator of Just Cause. In the case where the local church only has one elder and he is charged with a crime, the Chairman of the Region's Judicial Review Committee will appoint one of the committee's members to be the Moderator of Just Cause. Should the Moderator determine that there is enough evidence to establish just cause for a trial, either one of the local elders or the Chairman of the Region's Judicial Review Committee must file a corresponding charge (BCO-24.2.5) for a local or Regional Panel to evaluate. In the case where there is only one elder and the Regional Judicial Review Committee provides the Moderator of Just Cause, the Chairman of the Regional Judicial Review Committee will file a charge.

24.2.2 The qualifications of witnesses

24.2.2.1 Who Can Bring a Charge

A charge must be leveled by a member in good standing of a Sovereign Grace church.

24.2.2.2 The Qualifications of Witnesses

A credible witness, who is not a member of a Sovereign Grace church, can bring forward evidence of alleged criminal activity or scandalous sin that will be used in evaluating whether a charge should be brought against an elder in a Sovereign Grace church. The witness should bring their evidence to a member or elder of the local church where the accused elder currently serves. If there is only one elder in that local church, then the witness can bring their evidence to the Regional Judicial Review Committee. Contact information for the Regional Judicial Review Committee should be provided by the local church or the Regional Leader. If a credible witness, who is not a member of a Sovereign Grace church, doesn't believe sufficient attention was given to their evidence, they should contact the chairman of the Regional Judicial Review Committee to register their complaint. After the evidence is reviewed, and if a charge is to be brought against an elder, it must be leveled by a member, and/or elder in good standing of a Sovereign Grace church.

24.2.2.3 Two or More Credible Witnesses

No charge against an elder is to be admitted unless it is brought by the evidence of two or more credible witnesses (1 Tim. 5:19) (cf. introduction to BCO-24 above).

24.2.2.4 Witnesses of Character

Extra prudence is required whenever the plaintiff or a supporting witness is known to:

- Harbor ill will or a vengeful spirit against the defendant
- Be hasty in judgment or quick to accuse
- Lack integrity or a reputation for honesty
- Be under discipline or a process of discipline themselves
- Possess a conflict of interest or would benefit from the defendant being found guilty

24.2.2.5 Consideration and Care for the Witnesses

In some cases, the witness or individual bringing forward a charge has been wronged or is in a vulnerable position. Local elders have a responsibility to provide appropriate care for such an individual, to protect them from potential intimidation, etc.

24.2.3 Within Two Years of the Alleged Offense

Charges must be brought forward within two years of the alleged offense, unless it can be established that unusual circumstances prevented this (e.g. the offended party was a minor at the time, etc.). The two year limitation will be waived if the charge concerns sexual misconduct or criminal behavior. The eldership with original jurisdiction over the defendant has the power to determine if circumstances warrant waiving the two-year limitation period.

24.2.4 Counsel for the Plaintiff

It is likely that a congregant will talk to one of their elders about the possibility of bringing a charge against another elder. Under such circumstances, the elder shall recommend to the congregant a godly advisor (such as a small group leader, or perhaps a member of the Regional Judicial Review Committee) who can serve as a confidant and counselor during this difficult and confidential process. If the congregant cannot or does not wish to talk with one of the local elders about the possible charge, then the congregant should contact the Regional Judicial Review Committee. The Committee will then recommend a counselor.

24.2.5 Submitted in Writing

A charge must be submitted in writing by a member or fellow elder within Sovereign Grace. The charge shall be submitted first to the defendant and secondly to uncharged members of the local eldership. If there are no other uncharged members of the local eldership, then the Regional Judicial Review Committee has original jurisdiction in the case (cf. BCO-22.1) and the charge should be submitted directly to the Regional Judicial Review Committee. The charge should detail the following:

- 24.2.5.1 The alleged offense (A brief and simple description of alleged offense suffices);
- 24.2.5.2 Relevant Scriptures;
- 24.2.5.3 Relevant sections of the Sovereign Grace *Statement of Faith* or Book of Church Order;
- 24.2.5.4 Any effort(s) made by the plaintiff to make the elder aware of this deficiency and the response to these efforts;
- 24.2.5.5 Why the charge carries sufficient weight for a trial.

24.2.6 Sufficient Weight for a Trial

For a charge to be admitted and a trial called, there should be sufficient grounds regarding the seriousness of the offense. An admitted charge should represent a serious breach of *sound doctrine* (as defined by the Sovereign Grace *Statement of Faith*) or the *character qualifications* for office (1 Tim. 3:1-8; Titus 1:5-9; cf. BCO-3).

Thus, charges cannot be made because a member disagrees with the decisions or the "style" of the elder, with the doctrine of Sovereign Grace, or with doctrines not explicitly or implicitly addressed in the Sovereign Grace *Statement of Faith*. Such differences are part of every relationship and of normal church life and do not constitute a basis for charges against an elder.

Further, a charge must have sufficient evidence to be legitimate. Simple hearsay, where the plaintiff was not directly involved in a situation and only became aware of it through the reports of others, may warrant further investigation but is generally not sufficient by itself to warrant a charge.

24.3 Moderator of Just Cause Pretrial Procedures

When a charge is made against an elder at the local church level, the uncharged elders should appoint one of their number to be the Moderator of Just Cause in order to make the determination of whether or not there is sufficient justification for a trial. If, after appropriate recusals, there aren't enough remaining uncharged elders to serve as Moderator of Just Cause, then the Chairman of the Region's Judicial Review Committee should be contacted in order that he may appoint a Moderator of Just Cause from the Judicial Review Committee. The Moderator of Just Cause's responsibilities are:

24.3.1 To receive the formal, written charges directly from the accuser or the local elders who received the charge. Along with the charge, the accuser shall submit in writing a description of all the existing evidence that the plaintiff plans to bring forward in support of the charge. The written description should include information regarding the witnesses: their name(s), address or contact information, local church affiliation, a brief description of what they will share;

24.3.2 To communicate directly with the accuser until a Panel is appointed at which time the Moderator of the Panel shall communicate with the parties;

24.3.3 To make sure that the accuser has already fulfilled his/her responsibility in Matthew 18:15-16, including that a copy of written charges has already been presented to the defendant;

24.3.4 To make sure that the fundamental requirements for bringing a charge (BCO-24.2) have been met;

24.3.5 To inform the plaintiff of the seriousness of bringing a charge against an elder while not intimidating him/her;

24.3.6 To inform the plaintiff of the possible outcomes of bringing a charge against an elder and asking the plaintiff what outcomes he/she desires;

24.3.7 To ascertain if there are any witnesses who will substantiate the charge(s), identify those witnesses, and to personally talk to those witnesses to determine the nature and content of their testimony;

24.3.8 To determine, after examining the evidence, whether or not there is sufficient cause for a trial;

24.3.9 To recommend mediation instead of a trial to the plaintiff and the defendant if appropriate and mutually agreeable. If either party does not agree then the process proceeds to trial. If during an agreed upon mediation, should the defendant confess to and repent of the charges

PART FOUR – Rules of Discipline Section 24 – Discipline of an Elder

brought by the plaintiff and agree to the remedy sought by the plaintiff then the matter does not have to be adjudicated and the eldership will apply the appropriate result (BCO-24.9) and the matter is closed.

24.3.10 Once the Moderator of Just Cause has reached a determination he must communicate to each of the parties with a formal written decision using the format from Rule 40 of the *Rules of Procedure*. Decisions are not to be emailed. The summary of decision should be easily understood. The technical aspects of the decision should be left in the Basis of Decision.

24.3.11 If the decision is to go to trial, the Moderator of Just Cause will serve as an advisor to the person bringing the charge on procedural matters.

24.3.12 If the decision is to go to trial, the Moderator of Just Cause must inform the remaining elders of the local church, the Chairman of the Judicial Review Committee, and the Regional Leader.

24.3.13 Should the Moderator of Just Cause find that the charge has merit he will report such to the Chairman of the Judicial Review Committee and to the Regional Leader. The Regional Leader will conduct a blind draw to select a three-judge Panel to hear the case.

24.3.14 The Regional Leader will ensure that there is pastoral care for the defendant, and appoint an advisor/pastor to the plaintiff.

24.3.15 The Panel will then select one of their number to be the moderator of the Panel. He is responsible for communicating with each of the parties, ensuring that the minutes of the trial proceedings are being kept, that order is maintained, and that the *Book of Church Order* and *Rules of Procedure* for Adjudications are being followed.

24.3.16 The moderator of the Panel may hold a pretrial conference with the parties if he deems it necessary. There must not be ex parte conversations between the members of the Panel and the parties. Further trial direction and procedures are found in the *Rules of Procedure for Adjudications*.

24.4 Plaintiff May Appeal Moderator's Decision about Charge

If the Moderator decides not to admit the charge, the plaintiff may then appeal this decision within 30 days. An appeal is made by writing a letter of no more than five pages to the Regional Judicial Review Committee about why the Moderator has wrongly rejected this charge. The original written charge, written description of supporting evidence, the written response to the charge by the Moderator, and the written appeal will be mailed to chairman of the Judicial Review Committee. The member of the Regional Judicial Review Committee who served as the Moderator will be recused from deciding upon appeals related to the case."

The Judicial Review Committee will decide by majority vote if the decision of the Moderator is appropriate, if the charge should be heard, or if there is a third option for further action (such as mediation by a third-party, etc.). The response of the

Judicial Review Committee will be mailed to the plaintiff, postmarked within 30 days.

24.5 The Panel

The uncharged local elders who have received the charge shall recuse themselves if necessary. If there are only one or two local elders remaining to hear the case, they shall request from the Regional Judicial Review Committee the involvement of enough Committee members to constitute a three-person Panel (as per BCO-22.1.2). If there are no local elders left after recusals, then original jurisdiction of the case passes to the Regional Judicial Review Committee as per BCO-22.1.2.

24.6 The Rights of the Defendant

24.6.1 The Priority of Privacy

In most situations, the plaintiff and defendant should resolve the incident privately or among the local eldership.

Before this process escalates to the point of making an official charge, it is incumbent on the plaintiff and the elder to make all efforts to handle the situation face-to-face over a sufficient period of time. (N.B.: Victims of physical or sexual abuse are neither required nor advised to meet face-to-face with their abuser in this way). If an individual or party knows of the private offense of an elder, they should first approach the man in private, graciously bring their observation or charge, and call for repentance. If he fails to repent or persists in his sin, the charge should be brought to the attention of his eldership. In this case, we heed the wisdom of Paul that "love bears all things, believes all things, hopes all things, endures all things" (1 Cor. 13:7). We owe to one another the judgment of charity, assuming the best and seeking to resolve disputes and differences in a godly, humble, and patient manner. The process below occurs when such efforts have not satisfied the plaintiff.

24.6.2 The Priority of Pastoral Care for the Defendant

When an elder is accused, the Regional Leader shall have the responsibility to appoint an elder from either the church or from the Regional Assembly of Elders to provide pastoral care for the parties and their families.

24.6.3 The Priority of Confidentiality

There is to be a progressive involvement of other people, making nothing public until it is required by the process, and then only through the appropriate channels.

In Matthew 18:15-20, from which we derive our practice of church discipline, there is a progressive escalation of input if a person is not repentant. The matter is not told "to the church" (v. 17) until the person has refused the one-on-one appeal (v. 15) and the "one or two others" (v.

16). The church then makes an appeal through its representatives, the elders (v. 17). Only then is it appropriate to make a matter public. Until this point, the obligations of the Proverbs must be appreciated: "Whoever goes about slandering reveals secrets, but he who is trustworthy in spirit keeps a thing covered" (Prov. 11:13; cf. 10:18; 16:28; 18:8; 20:19; 26:20, 22).

The reputation of an elder is not to be damaged lightly. Secrecy and covering of scandal and sin is not excusable. However, Scripture is careful to protect leaders from hasty judgment and false reports (1 Tim. 5:19). Confidentiality should be carefully ensured until such a time as it is necessary to communicate publicly.

In the event of a public offense (BCO-24.2.1.1) that is also scandalous in nature, particularly if it is both criminal and public, the local eldership will seek input from the Chairman of the Judicial Review Committee concerning communications to the church about the process and status of the disciplinary process. Protecting the defendant's rights to due process must be maintained, but caring for the church will require some communication when the matter is already public. Exceptions to rules regarding the timing of such communications, as described in the *Book of Church Order* (e.g., BCO-24.2.5; 24.6.6) and the *Rules of Procedure* (34.8), may be adjusted at the discretion of the Chairman, for the sake of caring for the church.

24.6.4   The Right to Face Your Accuser

The accused elder has the right to face his accuser, unless the charge stems from the testimony of a minor.

It is a grave thing to bring a charge against a leader of God's people, and the accuser should be aware that he/she will have to give account before God for his/her testimony (Deut. 19:15-19, cf. Deut. 17:7). The accuser should be made aware of the weight of the testimony he/she is giving.

24.6.5   The Wife of the Defendant

The wife of the defendant elder is not required to testify against her husband. She can serve as a witness if she so chooses, but this is not mandated.

24.6.6   Due Process

Due process must be followed and a presumption of innocence granted until judgment is rendered by the Panel. Public pronouncements about a pastor's qualifications must not be made until after the Panel issues its decision.

24.6.7 Appeal

If found to be at fault, the defendant has 30 days to file his formal appeal with his regional Judicial Review Committee. If the elder's ordination has been revoked, then the eldership may continue to pay him until the appeals process is over, but it is not required to do so.

24.7 The Rights of the Plaintiff

24.7.1 The Right to Make a Charge and Have the Charge Evaluated

Individuals have the right to make a charge against an elder, provided they meet the requisite requirements of Scripture (e.g. 1 Tim 5:19) and the *Book of Church Order*. When an individual or group brings a charge forward against an elder, they are afforded the right to have that charge evaluated by the other elders of the local church. However, this does not imply that the matter must go to trial. The Moderator must still determine if there is just cause for admitting the charge (BCO-24.3 above).

24.7.2 The Right to Confidentiality

There is to be a progressive involvement of other individuals, making nothing public until it is required by the process, and then only through appropriate channels.

Similar to the protections of the defendant spelled out above, Matthew 18:15-20 should guide a careful and deliberate escalation of input. The defendant, local eldership, and other involved parties must be careful to avoid making details public before it is required by the process. In particular, the plaintiff has the right to have their reputation protected. Effort must be made by the local eldership to ensure that the plaintiff does not become the object of retribution in the form of intimidation, slander, or gossip. In the same way that the defendant elder's reputation should be protected from hasty judgment, the plaintiff should be afforded the same reasonable confidentiality until such a time as it is necessary to communicate publicly.

There may be some instances where the identity of the plaintiff or witnesses should not be made public: the individual(s) may be particularly vulnerable, a minor, etc. Such a determination will be made at the discretion of the Panel.

24.7.3 The Right to Appeal

If the plaintiff is not satisfied with the decisions or judgments of the Panel, they have 30 days to file formal appeal with the defendant's regional Judicial Review Committee.

Likewise, if the plaintiff is not satisfied with the decisions or judgments of the regional Judicial Review Committee, they have 30 days to file formal appeal with the Sovereign Grace Court of Appeal.

24.8 Trial Proceedings

The following trial procedures shall be followed by Regional Judicial Review Committees and the Sovereign Grace Court of Appeal when they have original jurisdiction in trial proceedings. However, whereas local Panels are required to reach a binding decision within ten days (BCO-24.9), the Regional Judicial Review Committees and Sovereign Grace Court of Appeal may have up to 30 days to reach a decision.

The Panel shall fix the date of the trial and inform all relevant parties in writing. If the defendant fails to appear without satisfactory reason for his absence at the pre-appointed time of the trial, a one-time continuance will be granted. If he fails to appear on the second date, the trial will proceed in his absence. The time allowed for setting the date of the trial will be determined by the Panel with due consideration for the circumstances.

Likewise, the date of any trial or appeal before the regional Judicial Review Committee or Sovereign Grace Court of Appeal will be set by the presiding judicatory, making due consideration for the circumstances. They will notify all relevant parties in writing. If the defendant fails to appear at the pre-appointed time, the trial will proceed in his absence.

24.8.1 Commitment to Confidentiality and Godly Speech

If a trial is to be held, it is wise to establish a degree of confidentiality. Given the wide range of situations, it is left to the presiding Panel to determine what level of confidentiality is possible and beneficial to the process of justice (e.g. when an accusation against an elder is publicly known, it may serve the congregation to know that a process is being engaged to investigate the truthfulness of the allegation). Effort should be taken to protect the involved parties from the needless damage that can occur when the suspicion of wrongdoing is unduly communicated to others. Keeping potentially hurtful disclosures to the minimum possible level, consistent with a fair, clean, and thorough proceeding, is appropriate in such difficult situations and to protect the reputation of both the plaintiff and defendant. Discretion should also be applied to ensure that no party feels unduly isolated from suitable counsel, care, and accountability during the course of adjudication.

Beyond mere confidentiality, a good faith effort should be made by all involved parties to promote and practice godly speech. Words and speech should not be used as weapons to assault any individuals involved in a matter of discipline. Rather, all involved parties should endeavor to ensure that their speech is in keeping with the ultimate goals of biblical justice and restoration, that it may give grace to those who hear (Eph 4:29-31). Care should be given to prevent speech or actions that undermine a fair and unbiased process of discipline and adjudication. In addition, the involved parties and local church should strive to prevent speech that might carelessly or deliberately incite a reaction, generate divisiveness, or inflame conflict.

After the trial has been held and the Panel has written their decision, the results of the case will be made known to the local church, the Regional Assembly of Elders, and the Sovereign Grace Director of Church Development. In this way, it becomes a public matter. This is true regardless of whether appeals are made. In some instances, the identity of the plaintiff or key witnesses should not be disclosed to the wider public. This determination will be made by the presiding Panel, Committee, or Court.

If the elder is found not guilty of the charges, the case in essence is a *private* matter between two Christians and is therefore not to be discussed unless absolutely necessary (e.g. when an accusation is already publicly known). To do so inappropriately would constitute gossip and slander.

24.8.2 Rules for Evidence

24.8.2.1 Written communication (as opposed to electronic)

Throughout the duration of the process detailed below, all official communication between the elders and the parties involved in the trial must be written and not electronic. Further, all communication regarding the case must be included in the final set of documents to be kept on file by the local church and Sovereign Grace. This is to prevent causing unnecessary harm and to eliminate a potential source of sin for those involved in the trial.

24.8.2.2 Preparation for the Trial Hearing
24.8.2.2.a If the Moderator deems, in a preliminary fashion, that the requirements for admitting the charge and establishing just cause (see BCO-24.2-3) have been met, the plaintiff will present the following to the Panel:
- The official charge;
- Information regarding witnesses: their name(s), local church affiliation, and an estimation of how much time each will need to give their testimony;
- Names and local church affiliation of any advisors to be present during the hearing.

24.8.2.2.b The defendant will present the following to the Panel:
- A plea in response to the charge (i.e., "Guilty" or "Not guilty");
- Information regarding witnesses: their name(s), local church affiliation, and an estimation of how much time each will need to share their testimony;
- Names and local church affiliation of any advisors present during the hearing.

24.8.2.2.c The Panel may reduce the amount of time to be given to a witness if it is excessive and would extend the trial unnecessarily.

24.8.3 Advisors for Each Party

Each party in the hearing is allowed to have one or two persons to assist and advise them during the proceedings (and throughout the entire process). Such advisors must be members in good standing of a Sovereign Grace church (unless prior approval is obtained from the Panel). Each party must absorb their own expenses for this (the local church will not pay the expenses of the elder on trial). However, if the elder is ultimately cleared of the charges, the local church should reimburse him for all expenses related to his defense. While the parties will represent themselves in the hearing, the advisors may be present to give them assistance.

A party may petition the Panel to have the advisor speak on their behalf if they feel unable to adequately represent themselves. The Panel is not obligated to accept this petition.

Further, as this is not a jury trial, the Panel has the responsibility to make sure that both sides are heard and adequately cross-examined.

24.8.4 A Court Reporter

If a local church can financially support it, it may be wise to hire a court reporter for the hearing and present a final manuscript of the proceedings. A recording of the hearing must be made. Only the Panel and adjudicatories which review the case on appeal may have access to the recordings or to any transcript kept by a court reporter. These records of the proceedings will be kept on file by Sovereign Grace for at least 20 years

24.8.5 Cross-Examination

The hearing will include cross-examination to see that all evidence and testimony is treated as fairly as possible. The Panel will be entrusted with the task of keeping this cross-examination patient, gracious, and as gentle as possible.

24.8.6 The Hearing

The Panel shall review preliminary information and indicate to the parties the anticipated length of the hearing. Parties are responsible for notifying their respective advisors and witnesses. The plaintiff and defendant will face each other during the hearing.

The role of the Panel in this hearing is to make sure that Christian civility is maintained, that the plaintiff is enabled to appropriately convey his/her concerns and charge(s), and that all testimony is sufficiently heard and cross-examined. The Panel can decide to refuse certain evidence if it is not seen to be relevant or is too weak to make the intended point. Justice and godliness are to be preserved for the final outcome but also throughout the process.

Those present at the hearing will be the Panel, the two parties (plaintiff and advisors, elder and advisors), and the court reporter. Witnesses will be present only during their testimony.

If a court reporter is not used, someone will be present to handle the recording of the proceedings.

A hearing should include *at least* the following:

24.8.6.1 Determining the moderator;
The moderator will be chosen from among the members of the Panel. He is responsible for ensuring that the minutes of the trial proceedings are being kept, that order is maintained, and that the *Book of Church Order* procedures are followed.
24.8.6.2 Opening statements for both parties, not to exceed 30 minutes each;
24.8.6.3 Time for both sides to present evidence and witnesses;
24.8.6.4 Time for both sides to cross-examine and make objections;
24.8.6.5 Time for the Panel to interact with evidence and witnesses, seeking clarification where necessary;
24.8.6.6 Closing statement for both parties, not to exceed 60 minutes each, unless extended by a decision of the Panel.

24.9 Trial Results

A binding decision should be reached in no more than ten days. This decision should be submitted in writing to all parties and the regional Judicial Review Committee by registered mail. The decision should *not* be communicated via electronic medium.

The following five are the possible results of a trial:

24.9.1 Cleared of Charges

The defendant is not found to be at fault or there is insufficient evidence to establish proof of guilt by clear and convincing evidence.

24.9.2 Private Rebuke

The defendant is found to be at fault, but the offense is not sufficient grounds for removal from office or it was not deemed appropriate to make the matter public, especially for one who is repentant (1 Tim. 5:20).

24.9.3 Public Rebuke

The defendant is found to be at fault, and the offense is serious enough to warrant public reporting but not sufficient grounds for removal from office, especially for one who is repentant (1 Tim. 5:20). The public or grievous nature of the sin, while not disqualifying, warrants a public reporting.

If the Panel recommends a temporary suspension of office or some kind of a leave-of-absence as elder, the hope is that the elder will be restored to office. It is different from the man being removed, immediately losing his office, and being terminated as a result. If he does temporarily lose his office and the elder desires to be restored, there will be a second appearance before the Panel at the end of the prescribed regimen before he can be restored as an elder. The particulars of the temporary-leave process, terms, conditions of restoration, and restoration may vary according to the situation, and so the details are left to the discretion of the Panel.

24.9.4 Removal from Office

The defendant is found to be at fault for an offense that warrants removal. Written and public explanation of the charges and grounds for guilt should be provided to the local church, the Regional Assembly of Elders, Director of Church Development, and Sovereign Grace. The elder may be repentant, but the scandalous nature of the sin still requires removal (e.g. serious criminal behavior, adultery, etc.). The elder's ordination is revoked in such a circumstance as well.

24.9.5 Church Discipline

If the defendant is found to be at fault and is not repentant, then the local elders must apply their church discipline process in an appropriate manner. This process may ultimately lead to excommunication if the defendant remains unrepentant.

24.10 Process for Care and Restoration

24.10.1 Removal from Office

In the case of removal from office, effort must be given to extend care and counsel to the convicted elder, his family, and the local church. The goal of all church discipline is ultimately repentance, reconciliation, and where possible, restoration.

The Regional Leader will be responsible for coordinating care, in concert with the appropriate local elders, even if a man has no desire to return to ministry at a future date. Reasonable time and effort should be given to caring for the man and his family as he transitions out of ministry. Particular attention should be given to the spiritual well being of the removed elder and his family. While they may be resistant to such care, a good faith attempt must still be made. In the end, it is important to recognize that although appropriate time and effort may be given, the man and his family might remain dissatisfied, unrepentant, or unreconciled.

Additionally, the Regional Leader will coordinate care and counsel for the local church and elders. The primary responsibility for leading the church through such a season falls to its local elders. However, extra assistance, counsel, and care should be extended by the Region of any church that has an elder removed or excommunicated.

The presiding judicatory (i.e. Panel, Judicial Review Committee, or Sovereign Grace Court of Appeal) responsible for handing down a judgment for removal from office will set the date for the restoration hearing as part of their initial decision. The purpose of this hearing is to decide if the terms and conditions for restoration, detailed in their judgment, have been met. The judicatory should exercise discretion when setting the date to ensure that there is sufficient time for a process of restoration.

24.10.2 Return to Office

If a man who has been removed from office desires to return as an elder in a Sovereign Grace church, he will take initiative to contact the Judicial Review Committee that had the original jurisdiction in concert with the appropriate church and her elders. Restoration implicitly assumes that a man desires to be restored. He must inform the Judicial Review Committee in writing of his desire to move forward with his restoration hearing at least one month in advance of the date set by the presiding judicatory in their original judgment.

Both the convicted elder and his local elders will speak at the restoration hearing. They will provide testimony to the Judicial Review Committee regarding the man's progress in repentance. Both sides may provide evidence (documents or testimony) that the terms for restoration have or have not been met. The same rules for evidence and cross-examination for the initial trial apply here. The opinions of the local elders about the man's qualification to be restored will be weighed appropriately by the Judicial Review Committee.

The Judicial Review Committee will render a *final* judgment recommending or denying restoration. If it believes progress is being made, but that more time is required, it *may* schedule a subsequent hearing and must articulate in detail the ongoing terms and conditions for restoration.

If the Judicial Review Committee rules a man fit to return to ministry, his ordination and good standing as an elder in Sovereign Grace will be reinstated.

It is possible the Judicial Review Committee may rule to restore a man, but they or the local elders find it inappropriate for him to return to his former position or church. In this case, the man's ordination and good standing are reinstated, and he will be put in contact with his Regional Leader and the Director of Church Development (or a representative working in his stead) to explore future ministry opportunities.

N.B. If the local elders feel that new areas of concern regarding a man's fitness for ministry have surfaced in the time between the Judicial Review Committee's initial verdict and the restoration hearing, they must make a second charge against the man for him to be disqualified or denied reinstatement on that basis.

24.11 Communication

Communication for the discipline of a qualified pastor will be handled by the local church, according to the wisdom of its eldership. The entire and unedited written decision of the Panel will be sent to the local elders, the Regional Leader, the Chairman of the Regional Judicial Review Committee and to the Leadership Team of Sovereign Grace Churches. An appropriate summary of the decision which includes the pertinent information will also be written by the Panel for distribution to the local church and the Regional Assembly of elders, and upon request, sent to other Sovereign Grace elders. Any elder from within the Region may request the entire and unedited written decision from the Regional Leader.

24.12 Appeals

Either the plaintiff or defendant may appeal the Panel's judgment to the Regional Judicial Review Committee within 30 days. The plaintiff or defendant may further appeal the decision of the Regional Judicial Review Committee to the Sovereign Grace Court of Appeal within 30 days. If the decision of a Panel is overturned by a Regional Judicial Review Committee, the local elders on that Panel also have the right to appeal the decision to the Sovereign Grace Court of Appeal. An adjudicating Panel may grant an extension to either party of up to 30 additional days to file an appeal if it deems it appropriate.

24.13 Removal of an Elder(s) for Deficiencies

While not a situation that falls under the jurisdiction of discipline, an eldership may remove one of its members from his position (not removing his ordination) for deficiencies in the performance of his duties. In particular, a man may be removed if he is shown to be deficient in the areas of leadership, care, or teaching. These grounds for removal are *not* of a moral nature and do *not* represent any deficiency of character, per se, and therefore do not impinge upon his ordination.

24.13.1 Removal by His Local Eldership

24.13.1.1 The grounds for such removal or repositioning include significant deficiencies in the performance of his duties, significant deficiencies in leadership, pastoral care, teaching and preaching, incompetence, or incapacitation and not on the grounds of scandalous sin or heterodoxy.

24.13.1.2 The local eldership shall work with the Regional Leader to evaluate the elder's opportunity for improvement before proceeding.

24.13.1.3 An elder who is so removed or repositioned, will maintain his ordination status within the Sovereign Grace Churches.

24.13.1.4 Right of Appeal

24.13.1.4.a If the elder believes the local eldership sinned against him, he will have the right to appeal to the Regional Judicial Review Committee.

24.13.1.4.b If the elder believes the elders did not follow the procedure outlined above, he has the right to appeal to the Regional Judicial Review Committee.

25 Regional Judicial Review Committees

25.1 Appointment of the Judicial Review Committee

The Nominating Committee of each Region puts forward names of candidates, each of whom must be confirmed by a simple majority of the Regional Assembly of Elders.

Members of the Judicial Review Committee will serve six-year terms with no term limits. If an elder resigns before his term is up, the Nominating Committee will appoint a replacement for the duration of the term, pending confirmation from the Regional Assembly of Elders by simple majority vote.

The Judicial Review Committee will consist of five to seven pastors in a Region, preferably from different churches, with each case heard by three members of the committee. Men are assigned to a case through blind draw. An elder can be exempted for various reasons from time constraints to conflict of interest. If necessary, Regional Judicial Review Committee members may be shared between regions and serve on Adjudication panels (BCO-13.2.2.6), if approved by the receiving Regional Assembly of Elders.

25.2 Powers and Responsibilities of the Judicial Review Committee

25.2.1 The Judicial Review Committee will serve as a resource for informal counsel to elderships walking through a 1 Timothy 5:19-21 proceeding at the local level. This is to ensure that the procedural elements of discipline are followed.

25.2.2 A local eldership will not publicly rebuke or remove an elder without the involvement and help of the Judicial Review Committee.

In these instances (BCO-25.2.1-2), the Judicial Review Committee is not weighing in on the guilt or innocence of the elder, but assisting to ensure that a fair and just process has been carried out according to the procedures spelled out in the Rules of Discipline.

25.2.3 The Judicial Review Committee will also serve as a body of appeal for church members who have been disciplined or removed from membership. The Judicial Review Committee must hear the appeal of any excommunicated member, if it is made within the allotted time frame.

25.2.4 If a charge is brought against an elder but is not admitted by the Moderator (BCO-24.4), the person bringing the charge may appeal to the Judicial Review Committee. The Judicial Review Committee will determine whether or not the case shall be heard by the local Panel.

25.2.5 The Judicial Review Committee will be a place of appeal for any elder who is removed by a local Panel. The Regional Judicial Review Committee must hear the appeal of any trial decision regarding an elder at the local level (if the appeal is made within the allotted time frame). This result will be a binding decision in which the elder in question is cleared of charges, privately or publicly rebuked, or removed from office.

25.2.6 The Judicial Review Committee will serve as the original adjudicating body for the trial of an accused elder in the case where a local eldership is too small to adequately deal with the matter (cf. BCO-22.1.2). In such a case, the Sovereign Grace Court of Appeal would handle any further appeal.

25.2.7 A local Panel has recourse of appeal to the Sovereign Grace Court of Appeal should they disagree with any judgment by the Judicial Review Committee that overturns their prior verdict. However, the decision of the Judicial Review Committee should be enacted, even while the appeals process continues.

25.2.8 When the Regional Judicial Review Committee has the original jurisdiction in the case of an accused elder when the local eldership is too small to adequately deal with the matter, once their Panel renders a decision, the execution of that decision shall be the exclusive responsibility of the unaccused local elder(s). Should there be no unaccused elders, the execution of the decision shall be the exclusive responsibility of the Judicial Review Committee.

25.2.9 Charges Against Extra-Local Leaders

Charges against extra-local leaders (Regional Leader, Executive Committee member, Leadership Team member) that pertain generally to their qualification as elders will be handled according to the usual chain of jurisdiction for an elder (BCO-22.1): local Panel, Judicial Review Committee, Sovereign Grace Court of Appeal. The evaluation and discipline procedures of pastors apply to all the aforementioned Sovereign Grace extra-local leaders. Charges of heterodoxy or sin that pertain uniquely to the performance of their duties as extra-local leaders will be handled by the Judicial Review Committee (with possible appeal to the Sovereign Grace Court of Appeal), in the case of Regional Leaders, or by the Sovereign Grace Court of Appeal, in the case of Executive Committee members or Leadership Team members. Any elder may bring such charges and submit them to the body with original jurisdiction. Furthermore, any member of the Council of Elders may move to bring such charges against Executive Committee members or Leadership Team members. If the motion is carried by a simple majority vote, the Sovereign Grace Court of Appeal must try the charges. Complaints merely about job performance are handled by the Regional Assembly of Elders (in the case of Regional Leaders) and the Executive Committee (in the case of members of the Executive Committee and Leadership Team).

25.2.10 Public Censure of an Eldership

  25.2.10.1 A Note on Original Jurisdiction

  The Regional Assembly of Elders has jurisdiction over all elderships within the region in matters pertaining to the ordination, doctrinal fidelity, and moral integrity of elders. In such matters, the Regional Assembly of Elders has authority for censure and to disavow an elder's ordination. ("Disavowal" means that Sovereign Grace revokes its approval of a man's qualification for eldership and no longer recognizes him as an elder.)

  Each eldership is under the jurisdiction first of the elders of their region as represented by the Regional Judicial Review Committee, and then secondarily to the Sovereign Grace Court of Appeal.

  25.2.10.2 Any member in good standing may level charges against their local eldership. Any appeal will be made following the chain of original jurisdiction.

  25.2.10.3 Likewise, if the Judicial Review Committee with jurisdiction over an *eldership* refuses to hear charges of a doctrinal or publicly scandalous nature and two Regional Assemblies of Elders bring charges, the Sovereign Grace Court of Appeal will pick up jurisdiction (See BCO-26.2).

  25.2.10.4 Circumstances Requiring Public Censure

    25.2.10.4.a Persistent deviation from the Sovereign Grace *Statement of Faith*
    25.2.10.4.b Divisive behavior (e.g., making or condoning charges against Sovereign Grace members outside of the appropriate church judicatories)
    25.2.10.4.c Outstanding and impenitent sin on the part of the elders
    25.2.10.4.d Persistent failure to uphold the Sovereign Grace Book of Church Order or the Sovereign Grace Partnership Agreement

  25.2.10.5 The Censure of an Eldership
    25.2.10.5.a Some cases may require an entire eldership be put on trial as a whole, instead of being tried as individuals (e.g., if the elders have been charged with covering up scandal for each other or have together embraced heterodoxy). In these instances,

the procedure for censuring an entire eldership will follow the process for censuring individual elders.

25.2.10.5.b If however an eldership does not follow the recommendation of a Regional Judicial Review Committee regarding an appealed excommunication (see BCO-23.2.4), no new trial is necessary. The censure may be issued as soon as the Judicial Review Committee determines that its recommendation has been rejected.

25.2.10.5.c A copy of the censure will be sent to all elderships in Sovereign Grace for them to communicate to their congregations as they deem appropriate.

25.2.10.6 The Removal of Censure

25.2.10.6.a When an eldership is censured, there should be consistent contact and prayer from fellow elders in the region.

25.2.10.6.b The restoration of a censured eldership may be initiated by the censured eldership or by the Judicial Review Committee that issued the censure.

25.2.10.6.c The Judicial Review Committee will meet with the censured eldership and will review the case to determine whether the censured party has shown sufficient repentance and change. An eldership that has been censured will be restored only if the Judicial Review Committee believes appropriate conditions have been met and that restoration will not harm the reputation of Christ and the church.

25.2.10.6.d Restoration will be accompanied by a prayer of thanksgiving to God for his grace, and the removal of censure will be communicated as broadly as the original censure.

25.2.11 Disavowal of an Eldership

25.2.11.1 Circumstances Requiring Disavowal

If the Judicial Review Committee determines that a censured eldership has not changed its offending behavior in a credible and timely fashion, it may propose that the Regional Assembly of Elders disavow the eldership (i.e., revoke its approval and recognition of the ordination of the elders in question).

25.2.11.2 Procedure for the Disavowal of an Eldership

If the Judicial Review Committee proposes the disavowal of an eldership, this proposal must be confirmed by a simple majority of the Regional Assembly of Elders. If the Regional Assembly votes to disavow the eldership, the Regional Assembly of Elders will assume pastoral responsibility for the church's members, as described in BCO-9.5.

If the Judicial Review Committee's proposal of disavowal fails to obtain the support of a simple majority of the Regional Assembly, the Judicial Review Committee can do the following:

25.2.11.2.a Rescind their prior judgment and remove the censure;

25.2.11.2.b Keep the censure in place until the eldership evinces change warranting a removal of the censure;

25.2.11.2.c Keep the censure in place and re-propose disavowal of the eldership to the Regional Assembly at a later time.

If a Regional Assembly rules to disavow an eldership, the eldership can appeal the ruling to the Sovereign Grace Court of Appeal.

If the Sovereign Grace Court of Appeal overturns the Regional Assembly's majority vote to disavow the eldership, the Regional Assembly may again vote to disavow the eldership when there is further evidence of the eldership's persistence in that behavior for which it was originally censured.

25.2.11.3 Removal of a Church

When a congregation or portion of a congregation continues to recognize as its pastors men who have been disavowed, or who have never been approved by the Regional Assembly of elders for ordination, by the judicatories of Sovereign Grace, it ceases to be a Sovereign Grace church. Under such circumstances, if necessary, the Regional Judicial Review Committee may officially declare the removal of the church from the Region and hence from Sovereign Grace. In case of such a declaration, the church forfeits all rights and responsibilities of membership in Sovereign Grace.

25.2.11.4 Communication of Disavowal
Notice and explanation of the eldership's disavowal will be sent to all elderships in Sovereign Grace for them to communicate to their congregations as they deem appropriate.

25.2.12 Sovereign Grace has no rights to a church's assets and will assume none of its liabilities.

25.2.13 Likewise, no local church will assume either assets or liabilities of any other Sovereign Grace church or Sovereign Grace, the Executive Committee, or the Leadership Team.

26 The Sovereign Grace Court of Appeal

26.1 Candidates for the Sovereign Grace Court of Appeal are drawn from the members of the Regional Judicial Review Committees. They are put forward by the Sovereign Grace Nominating Committee, and each member is individually confirmed by a simple majority vote of the Council of Elders (cf. BCO-15.3.4). Members of the Sovereign Grace Court of Appeal are called Appellate Elders.

    26.1.1 When an appeal is heard by the Sovereign Grace Court of Appeal, the Appellate Elders from the Region in which the charge originated will recuse themselves in order to prevent conflict of interest.

    26.1.2 The number of Appellate Elders will correspond to the number of Regions.

    26.1.3 These Appellate Elders will be appointed to six-year terms, with no term limits.

    26.1.4 When a case is appealed, three Appellate Elders will be assigned to determine whether they will hear the case.

    26.1.5 A blind draw will be used to assign three Appellate Elders to a case.

26.2 Responsibilities of the Sovereign Grace Court of Appeal

    26.2.1 The Sovereign Grace Court of Appeal has the right to review or not review cases that have previously been decided by a Regional Judicial Review Committee at their discretion, pursuant to appeal. Any decision of a Regional Judicial Review Committee may be appealed up to the Sovereign Grace Court of Appeal by either party to the decision, or by a Panel whose judgment has been overruled. However, in any case where the Regional Judicial Review Committee has assumed original jurisdiction and conducted a trial (see e.g. BCO-22.1.2, when not enough local elders are available to constitute a Panel), the Sovereign Grace Court of Appeal must hear the case if it is appealed. The Sovereign Grace Court of Appeal may not decline to hear the case.

    26.2.2 The Court has the right to uphold or overturn the decision of a regional court and is not bound to grant another trial.

    26.2.3 Censure or Removal of a Region from Sovereign Grace

        26.2.3.1 Circumstances requiring the censure or removal of a Region include:
            26.2.3.1.a Persistent deviation from the Sovereign Grace *Statement of Faith*
            26.2.3.1.b Persistent divisive behavior (e.g., making or condoning charges against Sovereign Grace members outside of the appropriate judicatories)
            26.2.3.1.c Unrepentant sin on the part of the elders

26.2.3.1.d Persistent failure to uphold the Sovereign Grace Book of Church Order or the Sovereign Grace Partnership Agreement

26.2.3.2 Charges against a region must be brought by ten members of the Council of Elders. Elders and elderships within a Region which register their dissent against the position or action of the Region will be exempted from censure or removal.

26.2.3.3 If the Sovereign Grace Court of Appeal decides to hear charges brought against a region, then after any necessary recusals, a blind draw will be used to assign five elders to the case. If less than five Appellate Elders remain after recusals, then all of them shall try the case.

The Sovereign Grace Court of Appeal will render one of the following judgments:

26.2.3.3.a Not Guilty
26.2.3.3.b Censure
26.2.3.3.c Removal

26.2.3.4 If the judgment is for censure, the Council of Elders will finalize or overturn the decision by a simple majority vote.

26.2.3.5 If the judgment is for removal, a two-thirds majority vote by the Council of Elders will finalize the decision of the Sovereign Grace Court of Appeal.

26.2.3.6 If the judgment of the Sovereign Grace Court of Appeal is not upheld by a two-thirds majority, it will immediately initiate a simple majority vote by the Council of Elders on whether to censure the Region.

27 Revision History

Any and all of the below revisions are binding and authoritative only from the date of their acceptance onward. No portion of the *Book of Church Order* shall be understood as binding in a retroactive way.

2013 - For all following amendments see Council of Elders minutes from October 29, 2013, available from Sovereign Grace upon request. *Roman numerals* refer to how the amendment was approved for the 1st Edition of the *Book of Church Order*, and the *BCO-numeric* references are where the amendments are reflected in the 2nd Edition of the *Book of Church Order*.

Amendments approved by the Council of Elders: III.A.2.b.iii. found in BCO-13.2.2.3; III.A.3.a. found in BCO-14.1; III.B.1.a-e. found in BCO-15.1.1-5; III.B.2.b.i.found in BCO-15.2.3; III.B.3.a. found in BCO-15.3.1; III.B.3.a.iii. found in BCO-15.3.1.3; III.B.3.j. found in BCO-15.3.10; III.B.4. found in BCO-15.4; III.E.4.f-g. found in BCO-18.4.6-7; IV.A.7. originally adopted as III.B.3.c.xi but was placed in this section by determination of the Polity Committee on Dec. 4, 2013. Found in BCO-21.7; IV.C.1-2. found in BCO-23.1-2; IV.D.2.b-f. found in BCO-24.2.3-7; IV.D.3-4. found in BCO-24.3-4; IV.D.5.a. found in BCO-24.5.1; IV.D.6.a. found in BCO-24.6.1; IV.D.7. found in BCO-24.7; IV.D.7.b.ii-iii. found in BCO-24.7.2.a-b; IV.D.7.d. found in BCO-24.7.4; IV.D.7.f. found in BCO-24.7.6; IV.D.11. found in BCO-24.11; IV.E.2.c-e. found in BCO-25.2.3-5; IV.E.2.h. found in BCO-25.2.8; IV.E.2.i.i. found in BCO-25.2.9.1; IV.E.2.i.v.2. found in BCO-25.2.9.5.b; IV.E.2.j.ii-iv. found in BCO-25.2.10.2-4; IV.F.1. found in BCO-26.1; IV.F.1.d-e. found in BCO-26.1.4-5; IV.F.2.a. found in BCO-26.2.1; IV.F.2.c-d. The amendment was to delete this section and add a sentence to BCO-26.2.1.; IV.F.2.e.iii. found in BCO-26.2.3.3.

2014 – For all following amendments see Council of Elders minutes from October 21, 2014, available from Sovereign Grace upon request. References refer to the 3rd Edition of the *Book of Church Order*.

Amendments approved by the Council of Elders: BCO-1.10.1 (footnote); BCO-9.3.9; BCO-9.4 from 2nd Edition was deleted; BCO-12.1; BCO-13.1; BCO-13.2.7.1.a; BCO-13.2.7.1.b; BCO-13.2.7.1.c; BCO-13.2.7.1.d; BCO-14.1; BCO-15.3.1.3; BCO-15.3.1.4; BCO-15.4.1; BCO-17.3 from 2nd Edition was deleted; BCO-18.1; BCO-18.4.1; BCO-18.4.2; BCO-18.4.4; BCO-18.4.6; BCO-23.1; BCO-24.1; BCO-24.8; BCO-24.8.2

2015 (April) – For all following amendments see Council of Elders minutes from April 23, 2015, available from Sovereign Grace upon request. References refer to the 4th Edition of the *Book of Church Order*.

Amendments approved by the Council of Elders: BCO-19.

Also, Letter of Intent removed and changes made accordingly (e.g., BCO-27 was formerly BCO-28).

2015 (October) – For all following amendments see Council of Elders minutes from October 26, 2015, available from Sovereign Grace upon request. References refer to the 5th Edition of the *Book of Church Order*.

Book of Church Order Amendments approved by the Council of Elders relate to the following sections: 9.3.6; 9.3.9; 13.1.3; 13.1.5-7; 13.2.1.4; 13.2.2.1; 13.2.5; 13.2.7.1.b; 13.2.9; 14.2.5; 15.3.1.1; 15.3.1.4; 15.3.3.4; 15.3.3.10; 15.3.8; 15.4.4; 15.4.5; 15.2.1; 15.3.2.8; 15.3.3.9-10; 18.3.3.3; 18.4; 18.4.5; 25.1

2016 (October) – For all following amendments see Council of Elders minutes from October 24, 2016, available from Sovereign Grace upon request. References refer to the 6th Edition of the *Book of Church Order*.

Book of Church Order Amendments approved by the Council of Elders relate to the following sections: 13.1.3; 13.2.2.1; 13.2.4.2; 13.2.7.2; 15.2.1; 15.3.6; 15.4.2; 18.4.6; 18.4.10; 19; 23.1; 23.2.1; 23.3; 24.1; 24.1.1; 24.2.1.4; 24.5; 24.6.2; 24.8.1; 24.9.5; 24.11; 24.12; 25.2.7

2017 (October and special meeting in June) - For all following amendments see Council of Elders minutes from June 15, 2017, and October 2, 2017, available from Sovereign Grace upon request. References below refer to the 7th Edition of the *Book of Church Order*.

Book of Church Order Amendments approved by the Council of Elders relate to the following sections: 1.10.1; 1.13; 9.3.6.3; 9.7-8; 12.1-3; 13.1.1; 13.1.4; 13.2.4.1; 13.2.5.1; 13.2.5.6; 13.2.7.1.e; 13.2.7.2.c; 15.2.1; 15.3.3; 15.4.2.1; 18.4.1.4; 18.4.10.3; 19.3; 20.3; 24.10.2 (removed)

2018 (October) – For all following amendments see Council of Elders minutes from October 1–2, 2018, available from Sovereign Grace upon request. References below refer to the 8th Edition of the *Book of Church Order*.

Book of Church Order Amendments approved by the Council of Elders relate to the following sections: 1.4; 9.1; 9.3.6.1; 9.3.6.3; 9.6; 9.7; 9.7.2; 9.7.4; 9.8.3; 9.9; 12.3; 12.4; 13.2.5.4; 15.1; 15.1.1; 15.2.2; 15.3.1.2; 15.3.1.4; 15.3.3.2.e.5; 15.3.3.2.g; 17.3.3 (removed); 17.3.5 (removed); 18.3.1; 18.3.3; 18.3.4; 18.3.4.4; 18.4.1.4; 20.4; 24.2.2.1; 24.6.6; 24.13.1.4

28 INDEX OF KEY TOPICS

References [e.g., (12.7)] refer to the respective place in the BCO

Book of Church Order, the Sovereign Grace – And member churches (1.10.1); and ordination of elders (9.3.6); and church bylaws (12); process of changing (15.3.3); and Revision History (27); and Polity Committee (15.3.1.3)

Bylaws – Consistent with *Book of Church Order* (12.1); written by each local church (12.1); examined by Regional Judicial Review Committee (12.1.3)

Church – Definition of and government of (1.1-1.13)

Church Adoptions – Steps involved (13.2.5)

Church Discipline – Principles of (21); and the local church (22); and church members (23); member appeals of (23.2); and discipline of an elder (24); and requirements for charge against an elder (24.2); and Moderator of Just Cause in Pretrial Procedures (24.3); and *Rules of Procedure* (21.7); and rights of defendant; plaintiff (24.6-24.7); and the Trial (24.8); and Trial Results (24.9); and Care and Restoration of the defendant (24.10); and Appeals (24.12)

Churches without elders – And care by Regional Assembly of Elders (9.5)

Church Planting – Steps involved (13.2.4)

Congregation – And accountability of elders (8.4); and equal status with elders (11.2); and unity of (11.3); and receptiveness to elder's teaching (11.3); and responsibilities of (11.4); and submission to elders (11.5)

Council of Elders – Definition of and makeup of (15.1); responsibilities of (15.3); committees of (15.3.1); and changing *Statement of Faith* (15.3.2); and changing *Book of Church Order* (15.3.3); and confirming Court of Appeals (15.3.4); and adjudicating charges against Region (15.3.5); and electing members to Executive Committee (15.3.6); and changes to Ordination Standards (15.3.8); and approving budget (15.3.9); and public statements (15.3.10); and meeting procedures (15.4); and Rules Committee (15.4.3)

Court of Appeals, Sovereign Grace – Candidates from Regional Judicial Review Committee (15.3.4); confirmed by Council of Elders (15.3.4); Appointment to (26.1); responsibilities of (26.2); actions against a Region (26.2.3)

Deacons – Definition of (10.1); characteristics of (10.2); and role of (10.3); and whether men or women (10.3)

Elders – Definition of (2.1); responsibilities of (2.2); biblical qualifications of (3); and his household (3.4); leadership gift (3.6); basis for removal (3.7); are Christians before they

Section 28 – Index of Key Topics

are elders (4); and plurality (5); and bi-vocational elders (6); and senior/lead pastor (7); and accountability (8); and ordination (9); discipline of (24)

Executive Committee – Council of Elders electing members (15.3.6); and selection to, responsibilities of, service on, and members of (17); and oversight of Leadership Team (17)

Executive Director – Council of Elders confirms (15.3.7); Definition of, responsibilities of, and place on Executive Committee (18.4.1); and Partnership Agreements (19)

Leadership Team – And Sovereign Grace Nominating Committee (16.3); Definition of, qualifications for, and mandate of (18); current Director positions (18.4); and accountability by Executive Committee (17)

Nominating Committee (Sovereign Grace) – Definition and makeup of (15.3.1.2); and Executive Committee (15.3.6); and purpose of, responsibilities of, and service on (16); and Regional Leaders (16.3)

Ordination of Elders – Basic process of (9.3); feedback in process of (9.2); and Pastors College (9.3.4); and ordination service (9.3.9); transfer between regions (9.7); transfer from other denominations (9.8)

Partnership Agreement – Of provisional regions (19.1); of United States churches (19.2)

Polity Committee – Definition and makeup of (15.3.1.3); and changes to Book of Church Order (15.3.3); and Rules of Procedure (15.3.1.3)

Region – Definition of (13.1); provisional regions (13.1.3)

Regional Assembly of Elders – Definition of (13.1.2); responsibilities of (13.2); and approving ordination candidates (13.2.1); and adjudications in the Region (13.2.2); and discipline of an eldership (13.2.3); and church planting (13.2.4); and church adoptions (13.2.5); and care for elders in Region (13.2.6); and main committees and ad hoc committees (13.2.7); and approving changes to *Statement of Faith* (13.2.8)

Regional Church Planting Committee – Definition and makeup of (13.2.7.1.c); and church adoptions (13.2.5)

Regional Judicial Review Committee – Definition and makeup of (13.2.7.1.b); and minutes of Regional Assembly of Elders (13.2.9); appointment to (25.1); responsibilities of (25.2); and church adoptions (13.2.5); and actions against an entire eldership (25.2.10-25.2.11); candidates for Court of Appeals (15.3.4)

Regional Leader – Definition of (14.1); responsibilities of (14.2); and qualifications of (14.3); and church adoptions (13.2.5); and Nominating Committee (16.3); and Partnership Agreement (19.1.4.2; 19.2.4.2); and churches separating from Sovereign Grace (20.2.1); and the discipline of an elder (24.1; 24.3; 24.10.1; 24.11; 24.13)

Regional Nominating Committee – And recommendations for Regional Committees (13.2.7)

Regional Ordination Committee – Definition and makeup of (13.2.7.1.a); and church adoptions (13.2.5); and ordination of an elder (9.3.3; 9.3.6; 13.2)

(Elder) Resignation Agreement (9.9)

Rules of Procedure – And the Polity Committee (15.3.1.3); and church discipline (21.7)

Senior/Lead Pastor – Definition of (7.1); Transition of (7.2)

Sovereign Grace Churches – Definition of (1.9-1.10); core values of (1.12); commission to disciple the nations (1.11); *Partnership Agreement* of member churches (19); and withdrawal from (20)

Statement of Faith – Member churches approve and appropriate (1.10.1); and ordination of elders (9.3; 13.2.1); and church adoptions (13.2.5); approval by Regional Assembly of Elders (13.2.8); process of changing (15.3.2); and Theology Committee (15.3.1.4); and Partnership Agreement (19); and withdrawal from Sovereign Grace (20.2.5); and charges against an elder (24.2.5; 24.2.6); and censure of an eldership (25.2.10.4); and censure of a Region (26.2.3.1.a)

Theology Committee – Definition and makeup of (15.3.1.4); and changing *Statement of Faith* (15.3.2)

Made in the USA
Columbia, SC
01 February 2019